SMALL STATES
& TERRITORIES
Status and Problems

UNITED NATIONS INSTITUTE FOR TRAINING AND RESEARCH

⌐SMALL STATES
& TERRITORIES
Status and Problems

A UNITAR Study
by Jacques Rapaport, *and others*
Ernest Muteba and Joseph J. Therattil

Contributions from The Division of Public Administration,
United Nations and Charles L. Taylor, Yale University

ARNO PRESS
A Publishing and Library Service of The New York Times

New York   1971

Copyright © 1971 UNITAR

*Published by permission of United Nations
Institute for Training and Research*

LC # 72-140128

ISBN 0-405-02237-9

Manufactured in the United States of America

CONTENTS

ANNEX

PREFACE

A study on the problems of small states and territories was planned in the very beginning of the Institute's research programme. The research design was submitted to the Board of Trustees in 1966 and was approved at the fourth session of the Board.

The study is concerned with the problems of very small states and territories, with special reference to the question of their role and participation in international affairs and the assistance which can be rendered to them by the United Nations family of organizations. The first part deals with the historical background of the problem and the issues raised by the participation of small states, as seen from the point of view of the international organizations, together with a discussion of the rights of the small territories. This part also seeks to explain the factors which have created or influenced the existence of these territories as separate international entities rather than components of larger political units. A second part analyzes the status of these states in terms of their political evolution and international relations, and then describes the various forms of foreign relations, participation in international and regional organizations, and security and military arrangements. This part is followed by a detailed examination of the practical problems of these states and territories in regard to public administration, viability, and other special aspects resulting from their isolation and limited population and education. The last part includes suggestions and proposals for international action, ranging from a better understanding of their acute and special difficulties to guarantees for security, economic and other assistance, and possible special United Nations services and aid.

The study has been carried out with the assistance and cooperation of officials of United Nations organizations and has benefitted from comments and suggestions by an international panel which met once in November 1967, half-way through the implementation of the project and, later in April 1969, to comment upon the final draft of the study. Those who participated in the panel meetings included Mr. A. Bozovic, Lord

9

Caradon, Mr. John Cates, Mr. M. E. Chacko, Professor Stanley A. deSmith, Mr. M. S. Esfandiary, Mr. Nikolai Fochine, Professor Roger Fisher, Mr. C. R. Gharekhan, Mr. V. V. Kuzmin, Mr. Arthur Lall, Mr. John Malecela, the late Dr. Z. K. Matthews, Dr. Arvid Pardo, Mr. Manuel Perez-Guerrero, Mr. Z. Seiner, Dr. Hans Singer, Mr. Constantin Stavropoulos, Professor Charles L. Taylor, Mrs. Patricia Wohlgemuth-Blair and Mr. Charles W. Yost. The Institute wishes to express its appreciation to these individuals, as well as to other officials who rendered assistance and cooperation.

This study was prepared by Jacques Rapoport with the assistance of a number of research associates, including Joseph Therattil, Ernest Muteba, James Freeman, Frank McDonald and Denise Wyns, with the guidance of the Institute's Director and Deputy Director of Research (Mr. Oscar Schachter and Professor Alexander Szalai). The chapter on Public Administration Problems was prepared by the Division of Public Administration in the United Nations Department of Economic and Social Affairs under the guidance of its Director, Mr. Chi-Yuen Wu. The statistics and typology on micro-states and territories annexed to the study was prepared by the Yale University World Data Analysis Program, under the direction of Professor Charles L. Taylor. The Executive Director notes most warmly the assistance received from these sources.

The Institute as such takes no position on the matters studied under its auspices. It, however, assumes responsibility for determining whether a study merits publication and dissemination. The views, interpretations and conclusions in this Study are those of the authors.

S. O. Adebo
Executive Director
May, 1970

INTRODUCTION AND BACKGROUND

A. INTEREST IN THE STATUS AND PROBLEMS OF VERY SMALL STATES

The existence of very small states which are fully or partially independent or of very small territories which want to attain a similar status is not a new phenomenon in international life. They have emerged, survived, disappeared, re-emerged throughout history in one form or another, and their right to existence has not been challenged very often in the past merely on the ground that they are too small to merit a separate existence. In fact, many have been integrated with bigger neighbours, or conquered by colonizers. However, a number of mini-states have survived and asserted themselves, and a surprisingly large number are now in the process of emerging from a twilight zone of semi-separate or dependent existence.

In the past, very small states played a leading rôle, more than once, in world affairs. The Republic of Venice was a world power in the 15th century, with a population under 150,000. It was also considered quite normal in the past to let small and insignificant states participate in world conferences. All the states of Europe which had participated in the war had the right to send plenipotentiaries to the Congress of Vienna in 1814-1815, which meant that innumerable minor powers were represented, including scores of independent German and Italian mini-states.

Well-established small European states have existed for a long time, without arousing any special controversy: Luxembourg, Iceland, Monaco, Liechtenstein, San Marino, etc. Some of them, such as Luxembourg, were members of the League of Nations and are Members of the United Nations; others are members of some of the specialized agencies or are parties to the Statute of the International Court of Justice.

The element of smallness *per se* did not give rise to much concern or study. Apart from monographs on specific territories, interest usually centred on problems common to territories small and large: political questions, such as colonialism and self-determination; economic questions, such as development; social problems, such as race relations;

11

educational problems, such as the brain drain, etc.

Interest in the consequences of smallness is a relatively new field, not only in the academic world,[1] but also in the forum of international organizations.

A first difficult question is that of defining smallness: where does smallness begin and where does it end?

Should the criteria be population, area, density of population, resources, isolation, or a combination of these elements, or is it unnecessary to bother about a definition, and qualify as small those countries and territories which consider themselves, and which the rest of the world considers, small?

A second problem is what kind of independence a small state can enjoy, politically and economically. Is the sole ultimate solution for a small country to integrate politically or economically or both with a larger unit, and under what conditions can it retain its separateness?

Thirdly, is it justified to look at small states and territories as a genuine category deserving examination, or are the situations so diverse that they have nothing in common but a meaningless smallness and therefore it serves no useful purpose to study their problems jointly?

Finally, if there is such a category as small states and territories with a minimum of specific characteristics and problems, how do they fit in the international picture, and what rôle can they play in international life?

The international problems raised by the existence of small territories can be examined from two different angles. On the one hand, from the point of view of the international organizations, the question arises whether they are really fully qualified as members and participants, and whether their proliferation is a reason for concern, particularly in regard to the decision-making procedures of these organizations. On the other hand, from the point of view of the small territories themselves, it is necessary to examine whether international action is required to protect their rights, define their duties and solve some of their difficulties.

B. THE PROBLEM OF THE PARTICIPATION OF VERY SMALL STATES IN INTERNATIONAL ORGANIZATIONS AS SEEN FROM THE POINT OF VIEW OF THESE ORGANIZATIONS

The question of the membership of very small states in the League of Nations, the United Nations and other international organizations is examined in a later chapter of this study.[2]

The few old mini-members of the family of United Nations organizations belong to the Western world (e.g. Luxembourg and Iceland, in

---

[1] One of the first books to appear on this subject is *Problems of Smaller Territories* edited by Burton Benedict, and published for the Institute of Commonwealth Studies by the University of London, The Athlone Press, 1967.

[2] See Part II, Chapter Two, Section C.

the case of the United Nations; Monaco, Liechtenstein and San Marino, in the case of other international organizations or programmes). There were very few of them. Why should their paradoxical equality with the super-powers be more questionable than the same principle applied to well-established larger, but still rather small states, for example the Central American republics? Even the entry into the United Nations, as a result of decolonization prior to 1960, of a few small under-developed countries, did not seem to raise any fundamental problem. But after the massive decolonization that followed, many small and under-developed countries joined the United Nations family. It was then suddenly realised that the composition of the international organizations was undergoing a radical change, that the possible combinations of votes which could produce majorities increased considerably, and that the relationship between decision-making and degree of financial contribution was changing radically.[3]

It should be noted, however, that most of the new Members of the period 1960-65 had populations over one million inhabitants, with the exceptions of Congo (Brazzaville), Cyprus, Gabon, Kuwait, Malta and Trinidad and Tobago. However, the successful applications for membership in 1965 of The Gambia (300,000 inhabitants, 10,369 sq. km.) and the Maldive Islands (90,000 inhabitants, 298 sq. km.) raised more acutely the question of the size of new Members. Would it still be possible to draw the line somewhere? Was the membership explosion beyond control, as dozens of smaller and smaller territories and islands were on the threshold of independence? From then on the problem of the "mini-states" or "micro-states" became a current and fashionable topic of discussion and articles.[4]

In recent years the question of the membership in the United Nations of micro-states has been twice raised by the Secretary-General[5] in no uncertain terms. But there has been a certain reluctance to take the matter up.

No guidelines have been proposed by the League of Nations or the United Nations as to the lower limits for membership, but various suggestions have been advanced informally on the subject of limited membership formulas for very small states: membership without vote, associate membership, group membership. It has also been suggested that

---

[3] For example, General Assembly resolution 2248 (S-V) of 19 May 1967, establishing a United Council for South-West Africa (Namibia), was adopted by 85 votes to 2, with 30 abstentions and 5 absentees. Contributions to the United Nations budget were as follows: 85 yes: 19.02 per cent; 2 no: 0.67 per cent; 30 abstentions: 80.11 per cent; 5 absentees: 0.20 per cent.

[4] A good example is F. Plimpton's article in *The New York Times Magazine* of 18 September 1966. See also *Proceedings of the American Society of International Law*, April 1968, pp. 155-188.

[5] See below, pp. 121-123.

the possibilities be explored of limiting the participation of small states by restricting it to cases where a direct or special interest exists; or to participation limited to subordinate or specified organs; or granting only consultative or observer status. Other suggestions have been made to the effect that the problem might be solved by dissociating the principle of sovereign equality from that of equal voting: this would open the way to weighted voting systems,[6] double majorities systems, etc.

The view that there might be something basically wrong in the unlimited acceptance of mini-states in the United Nations family has been expressed in various ways and in various quarters. A representative of one of the founding Members of the United Nations is reported as having said:

> It was not anticipated, nor, I believe, would it have been accepted in 1945 that the United Nations be extended to include tiny states whose only justification for existence is that their territory is no longer wanted by the colonial governments that for years supported them.[7]

The former permanent representative of Mauritania wrote:

> It is therefore understandable to those of us from smaller nations that the large countries see an injustice in the fact that one hundred million citizens of the world should be represented in the world parliament that the United Nations wants to be in the same manner as half a million of their fellow citizens. . . . Until this situation is remedied and the voice of each delegate justly represents the population and economic weight of his nation, the United Nations will not be effective.[8]

But contrary views have also been expressed. Some of these are indicated below as a matter of illustration, although it is not the purpose of this study to examine their validity. It has been stressed that the United Nations is not a world government, and that the General Assembly can only make recommendations, the real force of which lies in the weight of universal international public opinion. Therefore, the more universal the participation in the United Nations, the better, even if it is based on the principle of sovereign equality of widely unequal states, including mini-states. The Charter contains a built-in safeguard against General Assembly majority domination for those matters of importance which belong to the sphere of competence of the Security Council.

It has also been contended that small states are an asset for international organizations, precisely because they are small and weak,

---

[6] Studies have been made on weighted voting in the United Nations, and it has been suggested that such a system might solve the present mini-state problem. See *Mathematical Studies of Weighted Voting at the United Nations,* by Hanna Newcombe and Michael Silbert.

[7] *The New York Times,* 24 October 1966.

[8] *Jeune Afrique,* 23 October 1966, and *War/Peace Report,* April 1967.

and that their survival as independent entities depends more on respect for international law and the practice of international co-operation, than is the case for bigger states. It has been added that if, in addition to size *per se*, full, unadulterated independence and a minimum of political stability and economic viability are made the condition of true ability to carry out the Charter obligations, the number of qualified members of international organizations would shrink spectacularly.

On the other hand, the opinion that the addition, at this stage, of a score or more mini-members would seriously jeopardize the United Nations or other international organizations is not taken too seriously by all. On many issues (designed to influence international opinion, and to build up pressures, but not generate specific international action), the pattern of majority recommendations would probably not be substantially changed. And on matters of action, entailing serious consequences, the weight of the views strongly held by the great powers would probably not be seriously impaired.

Some consider that a study of the eligibility of very small states for membership in international organizations, with a view to barring some of the newcomers on the basis of their inadequate sovereignty or size or population or resources, would be an academic and impractical exercise at this time, when a number of very small states are already firmly entrenched and accepted members of the family. Fundamental changes in the membership provisions of the Charter of the United Nations and the specialized agencies are not likely to be seriously considered in the foreseeable future. Mini-states (or for that matter not so small, but poor and under-developed states) can play a constructive rôle in international organizations.[9] They may wish to exercise a certain amount of self-restraint in their activities, avoid overextending themselves, and accept certain organizational procedures which would alleviate the burden of their participation. International organizations could make a significant and specific contribution to the advantage of very small Member States if it is agreed to consider them as a specially deserving category.[10]

---

[9] The Prime Minister of Lesotho, speaking in the General Assembly, stated: "May I at this stage venture to speak for all the smaller countries, including those which have recently been somewhat derisively categorized as the 'mini-states.' Implicit in this description is the suggestion that they have no place in the international community, that they should forthwith surrender sovereignty and national identity and accept incorporation in some large political entity. I have three comments to make upon that view. The first, as I have already indicated, is that my people did not struggle for over a hundred years to achieve anonymity and oblivion. Secondly, I believe that such a view does not truly reflect the collective opinion of this Assembly and that it would violate the spirit and intention of the Charter. Thirdly, I believe that the smaller states have a specific and vital contribution to offer in the field of international relations" (A/PV.1565, p. 11, 25 September 1967).

[10] This idea has been occasionally expressed in United Nations debates.

In the following chapters this study will concentrate on these more positive approaches to the problem of the participation of mini-states or mini-territories in international life, rather than concentrating upon the more narrow issue of admission of small states to international organizations.

C. SMALL TERRITORIES AND THE UNITED NATIONS

It is one of the ironies of history that the attainment of independence by many mini-states and their admission to the United Nations should in some measure be due to the decolonization policies of the United Nations itself, whereas this proliferation of new members is considered by some as undesirable for the Organization.[11] The mini-states have never been the main objects of decolonization, of course; they are merely a logical and unavoidable result of a long evolution.

Without attempting to analyze the history of decolonization and the rôle of the United Nations, it should be recalled that the United Nations has been deeply involved since its inception in the struggle for self-government and independence for dependent territories.

Early in its history, the United Nations played a decisive rôle in the post-war emergence of colonial countries such as Indonesia, and the Organization devoted more and more time and effort to the decolonization process.

The regular activities of the United Nations, under Chapter I of the Charter, covered all the "Non-Self-Governing Territories." Using the information received on these territories under Article 73 e of the Charter, Committees of the General Assembly have scrutinized their affairs since 1946 and tried to influence their evolution towards self-government. Under Chapter XII of the Charter, the Trusteeship Council and the General Assembly, through the annual examination of reports and petitions, the despatch of visiting missions, and the supervision of elections and plebiscites, have played a direct role in the attainment of independence by eight of the eleven Trust Territories.

The most recent expression of United Nations policy on decolonization in general is to be found in resolution 1514 (XV) of 14 December 1960 (Declaration on the Granting of Independence to Colonial Coun-

---

Lord Caradon (United Kingdom), speaking about the small islands in the Caribbean, stated in the Committee of Twenty-Four: "Is it possible that the United Nations may play a new part, with new methods, in finding for these small territories, with their small populations, a place in the world in which the United Nations might perhaps provide assistance and guarantee?" (A/AC.109/PV.506, p. 13, 23 March 1967).

[11] However, the existence of micro-states and mini-territories as separate entities is due to historical factors which are much older than the United Nations. See Part I, Chapter Two.

tries and Peoples). The operative paragraphs of this resolution read as follows:

> [*The General Assembly*] *Declares* that
> 1. The subjection of peoples to alien subjugation, domination and exploitation constitutes a denial of fundamental human rights, is contrary to the Charter of the United Nations and is an impediment to the promotion of world peace and co-operation;
> 2. All peoples have the right to self-determination; by virtue of that right they freely determine their political status and freely pursue their economic, social and cultural development;
> 3. Inadequacy of political, economic, social or educational preparedness should never serve as a pretext for delaying independence;
> 4. All armed action or repressive measures of all kinds directed against dependent peoples shall cease in order to enable them to exercise peacefully and freely their right to complete independence, and the integrity of their national territory shall be respected;
> 5. Immediate steps shall be taken, in Trust and Non-Self-Governing Territories or all other territories which have not yet attained independence, to transfer all powers to the peoples of those territories, without any conditions or reservations, in accordance with their freely expressed will and desire, without any distinction as to race, creed or colour, in order to enable them to enjoy complete independence and freedom;
> 6. Any attempt aimed at the partial or total disruption of the national unity and the territorial integrity of a country is incompatible with the purposes and principles of the Charter of the United Nations;
> 7. All States shall observe faithfully and strictly the provisions of the Charter of the United Nations, the Universal Declaration of Human Rights and the present Declaration on the basis of equality, non-interference in the internal affairs of all States, and respect for the sovereign rights of all peoples and their territorial integrity.

The far-ranging scope of the principles contained in this resolution is underscored by the use of the word "all" in paragraphs 2 and 5, and the drafting of paragraph 3.

From the beginning until fairly recently, the decolonization effort in the United Nations has been aimed at relatively large territories or areas with a more or less sizeable population. The majority of these territories are now independent, but the stress is still on the remaining large colonial areas in Southern Africa: Angola, Mozambique, Southern Rhodesia, Namibia (South-West Africa). However, in recent years, the pressure for decolonization has logically extended to smaller and smaller territories, now constituting the bulk of the "remnants of Empires."

No systematic attempt seems to have been made to consider the possible philosophical, legal or other justification for limitations to the right to independence of territories with very small area or population.[12] On the contrary, the Special Committee of Twenty-Four (which since 1961 has been the organ of the General Assembly dealing with decolonization) stated in its 1964 report[13] that it was convinced that the provisions of the Declaration were fully applicable to smaller territories in the Atlantic or Pacific Ocean areas and in the Caribbean. And General Assembly resolution 2105 (XX) of 20 December 1965 contained a request to the Special Committee of Twenty-Four

> to pay particular attention to the small territories, and to recommend to the General Assembly the most appropriate ways, as well as the steps to be taken, to enable the populations of these territories to exercise fully their right to self-determination and independence.

General Assembly resolutions 2189 (XXI), para. 16 of 13 December 1966 and 2326 (XXII), para. 17 of 16 December 1967 contain the same language.

However, the question of drawing the line somewhere is raised occasionally in private utterances, and it has been asked more than once whether Pitcairn Island, with a population of 86, enjoys the inherent right to become an independent state.

It should be pointed out that when the General Assembly adopted the Declaration on the Granting of Independence to Colonial Countries and Peoples, in December 1960, it also adopted the next day, on 15 December 1960, a resolution 1541 (XV) on "Principles which should guide Members in determining whether or not an obligation exists to transmit the information called for under Article 73 e of the Charter" (in other words, in determining whether a territory is still under full colonial rule or not). Resolution 1541 (XV) is not particularly concerned with small territories. It has a long history predating the immediate origins of resolution 1514 (XV) (Declaration on the Granting of Independence to Colonial Countries and Peoples). As early as 1953, a list of factors "indicative of the attainment of independence or of other separate systems of self-government" was drawn up to be used in determining whether or not any territory was or no longer was within the scope of Chapter XI of the Charter.[14] At that time, the main consideration was to establish guidelines about the discontinuation of the transmission of information.

In 1960, the General Assembly was less concerned about discontinu-

---

[12] The Special Committee on Principles of International Law concerning Friendly Relations and Co-operation between States discussed "the principle of equal rights and self-determination of peoples," but the matter of size of population or of territory was not raised (A/6799, paras. 171-235).

[13] A/5800/Rev.1, Chapter I, para. 164.

[14] General Assembly resolution 742 (VIII) of 27 November 1953 indicates that the following factors should be used as a guide:

ation of transmission of information than with the refusal of certain powers (in particular, Portugal) to recognize the non-self-governing character of some of their overseas territories.

I. *Factors indicative of the attainment of independence or of other separate systems of self-government*
   A. International status
      1. International responsibility
      2. Eligibility for membership in the United Nations
      3. General international relations
      4. National defense
   B. Internal self-government
      1. Form of government
      2. Territorial government
      3. Economic, social and cultural jurisdiction
II. *Factors indicative of the attainment of other separate systems of self-government*
   A. General
      1. Opinion of the population
      2. Freedom of choice
      3. Voluntary limits of sovereignty
      4. Geographical considerations
      5. Ethnic and cultural considerations
      6. Political advancement
   B. International status
      1. General international relations
      2. Change of political status
      3. Eligibility for membership in the United Nations
   C. Internal self-government
      1. Territorial government
      2. Participation of the population
      3. Enocomic, social and cultural jurisdiction
III. *Factors indicative of the free association of a territory on equal basis with the metropolitan or other country as an integral part of that country or in any other form*
   A. General
      1. Opinion of the population
      2. Freedom of choice
      3. Geographic considerations
      4. Ethnic and cultural considerations
      5. Political advancement
      6. Constitutional considerations
   B. Status
      1. Legislative representation
      2. Participation of the population
      3. Citenship
      4. Government officials
   C. Internal constitutional conditions
      1. Suffrage
      2. Local rights and status
      3. Local officials
      4. Internal legislation
      5. Economic, social and cultural jurisdiction

The General Assembly adopted certain principles[15] to determine whether a territory was or was not self-governing, whatever the views of the administering Power might be. According to these criteria, it would be

[15] General Assembly resolution 1541 (XV) of 15 December 1960:

Principle IV: *Prima facie* there is an obligation to transmit information in respect of a territory which is geographically separate and is distinct ethnically and/or culturally from the country administering it.

Principle V: Once it has been established that such a *prima facie* case of geographical and ethnical or cultural distinctness of a territory exists, other elements may then be brought into consideration. These additional elements may be, *inter alia,* of an administrative, political, juridical, economic or historical nature. If they affect the relationship between the metropolitan State and the territory concerned in a manner which arbitrarily places the latter in a position or status of subordination, they support the presumption that there is an obligation to transmit information under Article 73 e of the Charter.

Principle VI: A Non-Self-Governing Territory can be said to have reached a full measure of self-government by:

(a) Emergence as a sovereign independent State;

(b) Free association with an independent State; or

(c) Integration with an independent State.

Principle VII:

(a) Free association should be the result of a free and voluntary choice by the peoples of the territory concerned expressed through informed and democratic processes. It should be one which respects the individuality and the cultural characteristics of the territory and its peoples, and retains for the peoples of the territory which is associated with an independent State the freedom to modify the status of that territory through the expression of their will by democratic means and through constitutional processes.

(b) The associated territory should have the right to determine its internal constitution without outside interference, in accordance with due constitutional processes and the freely expressed wishes of the people. This does not preclude consultations as appropriate or necessary under the terms of the free association agreed upon.

Principle VIII: Integration with an independent State should be on the basis of complete equality between the peoples of the erstwhile Non-Self-Governing Territory and those of the independent country with which it is integrated. The peoples of both territories should have equal status and rights of citizenship and equal guarantees of fundamental rights and freedoms without any distinction or discrimination; both should have equal rights and opportunities for representation and effective participation at all levels in the executive, legislative and judicial organs of government.

Principle IX: Integration should have come about in the following circumstances:

(a) The integrating territory should have attained an advanced stage of self-government with free political institutions, so that its peoples would have the capacity to make a responsible choice through informed and democratic processes;

(b) The integration should be the result of the freely expressed wishes of the territory's peoples acting with full knowledge of the change in their status, their wishes having been expressed through informed and democratic processes, impartially conducted and based on universal adult suffrage. The United Nations could, when it deems it necessary, supervise these processes.

possible to judge whether a territory had or had not genuinely attained a full measure of self-government, particularly when it had not become fully independent. As will be seen later in the study of the mini-states, these principles are specially relevant for small territories.

As more and more colonial lands become independent, interest about the fate of smaller and smaller territorial units increased, and pressure to decolonize them built up.

In recent years, each time the Committee of Twenty-Four (the full name of which is "Special Committee on the Situation with Regard to the Implementation of the Declaration on the Granting of Independence to Colonial Countries and Peoples") has reviewed the situation of a specific small territory, it has consistently and increasingly stressed the right of the people of that territory to self-determination and independence, and has urged that steps be taken to translate these rights into realities.[16]

---

[16] A few excerpts taken from the resolutions of the 20th and 21st sessions of the General Assembly which had been adopted on the basis of the report of the Committee of Twenty-Four:

General Assembly resolution 2066 (XX) of 16 December 1965 on Mauritius
[The General Assembly] reaffirms the inalienable right of the people of the territory of Mauritius to freedom and independence in accordance with General Assembly resolution 1514 (XV); . . .

Invites the Government of the United Kingdom of Great Britain and Northern Ireland to take effective measures with a view to the immediate and full implementation of resolution 1514 (XV).

General Assembly resolution 2230 (XXI) of 20 December 1966 on Equatorial Guinea
[The General Assembly] reaffirms the inalienable right of the people of Equatorial Guinea to self-determination and independence in accordance with the Declaration on the Granting of Independence to Colonial Countries and Peoples contained in General Assembly resolution 1514 (XV); . . .

Requests the administering Power, in accordance with the wishes of the people of Equatorial Guinea to set a date for independence as recommended by the Special Committee . . .

Requests the Secretary-General to take appropriate action, in consultation with the administering Power and the Special Committee, to ensure the presence of the United Nations in the Territory for the supervision of the preparation for, and the holding of, the election envisaged in paragraph 4(b) above, and to participate in any other measures leading towards the independence of the Territory.

General Assembly resolution 2185 (XXI) of 12 December 1966 on Fiji
[The General Assembly] reaffirms the inalienable right of the people of Fiji to freedom and independence in accordance with General Assembly resolution 1514 (XV); . . .

Calls upon the administering Power to implement without delay the following measures:
(b) The fixing of an early date for the independence of Fiji.

General Assembly resolution 2226 (XXI) of 20 December 1966 on the Trust Territory of Nauru
[The General Assembly] reaffirms the inalienable right of the people of Nauru to self-government and independence; . . .

Although independence is mentioned only as one of the ultimate results of self-determination, it is accorded special importance. No territory should be deprived of its right to choose independence— whatever the circumstances.[17] And it is sometimes stated that even after a territory has ceased to be a non-self-governing territory and has attained full internal self-government, under the aegis of the United Nations, the Organization may continue to have a residual responsibility to ensure that the territory is guaranteed the right to choose full independence at a later stage;[18] this is the situation envisaged in General Assembly resolution 2064 (XX) of 16 December 1965 on the Cook Islands, after elections were held there in April 1965 under United Nations supervision and a constitution adopted in August 1965 giving the people of the Cook Islands (population 19,000) control of their internal affairs and of their future.[19]

The interplay of General Assembly resolution 1514 (XV) (emphasis on the right to self-determination and independence), and 1541 (XV) (self-government through a choice of alternative methods) has

---

Recommends that the Administering Authority should fix the earliest possible date, but not later than 31 January 1968, for the independence of the Nauruan people in accordance with their freely expressed wishes.

General Assembly resolution 2069 (XX) of 16 December 1965 on Islands in The Atlantic and Pacific Oceans and in the Caribbean

[The General Assembly] aware of the special circumstances of geographic isolation and economic conditions concerning some of these territories;

Calls upon the administering Powers to implement without delay the relevant resolutions of the General Assembly;

Reaffirms the inalienable right of the people of these territories to decide their constitutional status in accordance with the Charter of the United Nations and with the provisions of resolution 1514 (XV) and other relevant General Assembly resolutions.

[17] The Committee of Twenty-Four, reviewing the situation in islands in the Pacific, such as Niue, Tokelau, Gilbert and Ellice, Pitcairn, etc., "reiterated its view that the question of size, isolation and limited resources should in no way delay the implementation of the Declaration in these territories" (A/AC.109/L.485,L.486, L.487 and A/AC.109/PV.620, 11 July 1968).

[18] The Prime Minister of Jamaica stated in the General Assembly that "since the 19th regular session of the General Assembly, Jamaica has been calling attention to the need for the United Nations to have some residual rôle to play in the future of those [small and very small] territories which, having exercised their right of self-determination in accordance with resolution 1541 (XV) have chosen association with another state" (A/PV.1584, p. 17, 10 October 1967).

[19] General Assembly resolution 2064 (XX) of 16 December 1965, para. 6: "Reaffirms the responsibility of the United Nations, under General Assembly resolution 1514 (XV) to assist the people of the Cook Islands in the eventual achievement of full independence, if they so wish, at a future date."

been the subject of debate. The question has arisen in particular in connexion with the future of small territories. Some members of the Committee of Twenty-Four have argued that the provisions of General Assembly resolution 1514 (XV) relating to the right to complete independence were paramount and overshadowed the technicalities of resolution 1541 (XV). Others maintained that the alternatives offered in resolution 1541 (XV) were as important for the small territories as the general principles of resolution 1514 (XV). The discussion on this subject in 1965 was inconclusive, and was renewed in November 1966 (in connexion with the examination of the situation in the United States and British Virgin Islands) and in March 1967 (in connexion with the situation in the remaining islands of the British West Indies). Some representatives expressed the view that resolutions 1514 (XV) and 1541 (XV) were complementary; that full independence was not the only way in which resolution 1514 (XV) could be satisfied; and that it was not always feasible for "mini-territories" to have independence in the traditional way. But other members stressed the fact that the Declaration did not discriminate between the peoples inhabiting small territories and those inhabiting large territories, when it came to the question of the fundamental right of peoples to freedom and independence. These principles were equally applicable to all Non-Self-Governing Territories, irrespective of their size, their population or their economic and social conditions.

In fact, the difference is mainly one of emphasis and procedure rather than of substance, but this fact has been somewhat obscured in the passion and heat of the debates on colonialism.

The Committee of Twenty-Four has generally recognised that within the framework of the broad principle of the right to self-determination and independence, for all dependent territories, irrespective of size and population, there are special problems when a very small territory is concerned, and the United Nations has special responsibilities:

> The United Nations should take appropriate steps to ensure that the people of these [small] territories are enabled to express themselves freely on their future status and in full knowledge of the options available to them.[20]

Thus, there seems to be a consensus on the following two principles:

(a) the population of any dependent territory, whatever its size, has the inherent right to decide freely its destiny. This includes the right to choose independence, whatever the circumstances and consequences;

(b) the populations of dependent territories—and especially of very small territories—should have full knowledge of the options available to them, and of the advantages and difficulties of each formula of political status.

A reasonable extension of this principle is that this knowledge

---

[20] A/6300/Rev.1, pp. 769 and 770; A/6700/Add.14 (Part II), p. 237.

should also be available to territories which have already made a preliminary choice, but may still be looking for better solutions to their problems.

In addition, it is implied that the United Nations could be of assistance in tne implementation of these two principles in individual cases.

The *second principle*, that of enabling the peoples concerned to have an adequate knowledge of the options available to them, can only be applied if an adequate study is made of the various theoretical and practical options open to these territories. It may be of some interest to recall that, in one specific instance, United Nations assistance was requested to clarify the options open to a potential small state on the threshold of independence: in 1963, at the request of the Governments of Senegal and of the United Kingdom (on behalf of The Gambia), a United Nations team made a survey of the alternatives to association between The Gambia and Senegal. Similar United Nations assistance is conceivable in many other instances, but the administering Powers involved have shown little willingness to let the United Nations discuss the options with the peoples of their dependent territories.

As far as the *first principle* is concerned (freedom of choice), it is generally felt that United Nations participation in this process offers a desirable guarantee, and practice seems to bear this out. International involvement in plebiscites existed already prior to World War II (the Plebiscites in Schleswig, 1920; Allenstein and Marienwerder, 1920; Klagenfurt, 1920; Upper Silesia, 1921; Sopron, 1921; Saar, 1935), and after the war (Saar, 1955). The United Nations played a rôle in the Korean elections of 1948. The Organization was particularly active in plebiscites and elections in connexion with the attainment of independence of territories under the International Trusteeship System (Togoland under British administration, 1956; Togoland under French administration, 1958; Cameroons under British administration, 1959 and 1961; Western Samoa, 1961; Ruanda-Urundi, 1961); and more recently with elections in Non-Self-Governing small Territories: the Cook Islands, 1965; Equatorial Guinea, 1968.

The United Nations is already committed to similar activities in the future: the 1962 Agreement between Indonesia and the Netherlands on West New Guinea (West Irian) foresees an "act of self-determination" before the end of 1969, with the assistance and participation of the United Nations.[21]

A number of recent resolutions of the General Assembly and of the Committee of Twenty-Four recommended similar United Nations in-

---

[21] The "act of self-determination" with the assistance and participation of the United Nations took place in July-August 1969. General Assembly resolution 2506 (XXIV) of 19 November 1969.

volvement in the ascertainment of the wishes of the populations of remaining dependent territories, including potential mini-states.[22]

Recent resolutions of the General Assembly, many of which relate to small territories, may have given the impression that independence was the only way out of colonialism acceptable to the United Nations. This is not exactly so, although it is correct to state that from a United Nations point of view the right to self-determination is inalienable and that the possibility of opting for independence is pre-eminent. In other words, self-determination must be exercised without strings attached; at the time the people choose their new status, they have to be potentially independent, their choice must be unrestricted, and they may choose independence if they prefer, however small and poor their territory may be. In certain instances, however, the United Nations Committee on Decolonization expressed the view that it should be possible for certain small territories to unite with others in the area to form an economically and administratively viable state, and expressed regret that no effective steps had been taken to bring about a federation.[23]

Looking at the results of choices made with United Nations participation, it is interesting to note that the results were not always favourable to full independence and membership in the United Nations. In two instances only (Togoland under French administration and Ruanda-Urundi) of the United Nations supervised elections and plebiscites mentioned above has the operation resulted in full independence and membership in the United Nations; in one case (Western Samoa), the result was full independence without membership in the United Nations; in two instances, integration with another country (Togoland under British administration with Ghana; and the Northern part of the Cameroons under British administration with Nigeria); in one instance, federative arrangements (Southern part of the Cameroons under British administration with Cameroon); and in one case, a self-governing régime short of independence (Cook Islands).

The results were each time fully debated in the United Nations, but

[22] General Assembly resolution 2183 (XXI) of 12 December 1966 on Aden.

General Assembly resolution 2185 (XXI) of 12 December 1966 on Fiji.

General Assembly resolution 2228 (XXI) of 20 December 1966 on French Somaliland.

General Assembly resolution 2229 (XXI) of 20 December 1966 on Ifni and Spanish Sahara.

General Assembly resolution 2230 (XXI) of 20 December 1966 on Equatorial Guinea.

General Assembly resolution 2232 (XXI) of 20 December 1966 on Islands in the Caribbean and the Pacific.

[23] A/6700/Add.14 (Part II), para. 1033, p. 131 concerning the British Virgin Islands.

in none of these cases did the Organization question their validity, even if the cases did not entail complete independence and membership in the United Nations.

In other instances, the United Nations has attempted to ascertain *post facto*, but on the spot, the validity of elections bearing on the termination of a colonial régime in a small territory; this was done after Sarawak and Sabah (North Borneo) joined the Federation of Malaysia in 1963, rather than become independent mini-states.

In the past, the United Nations has even given its blessing to the termination of the colonial status of small territories by examining the facts *post facto* and in New York only; in 1953, when it recognized that the people of the Commonwealth of Puerto Rico had achieved a new constitutional status and had effectively exercised their right to self-determination;[24] in 1954, when it accepted that Greenland had become an integral part of the Kingdom of Denmark;[25] in 1955, when it accepted the new federal status of the Netherlands Antilles and Surinam in the Kingdom of the Netherlands;[26] and in 1959, when it accepted that the people of Alaska and of Hawaii had exercised their right of self-determination and joined the United States as equal States of the Union.[27] In these resolutions, the General Assembly congratulated the people of the Non-Self-Governing Territories in question and the colonial authority for these acts of self-determination and decolonization.

Some might say that this would not have been possible after 1960, because the anti-colonial atmosphere in the Organization has become more pronounced and the expanded membership has resulted in a more uncompromising majority. They cite as a proof the fact that attempts have recently been made to reopen the question of Puerto Rico. It may well be that from now on the United Nations will no longer give its blessing to an act of self-determination short of accession to full independence, without having been a party or witness *in loco* to the exercise of this right. But there is nothing to show that a majority would not go along with forms of decolonization other than attainment of full independence if it is satisfied that this is really the clearly expressed wish of the population.

In the case of the change of status of six small British islands in the Caribbean (Antigua, Dominica, Grenada, St. Kitts-Nevis-Anguilla, St. Lucia and St. Vincent), the Committee of Twenty-Four debated not so much the question as to whether the new status went far enough (it falls short of independence but each island can unilaterally opt for full independence under certain conditions), but the fact that the status had

[24] General Assembly resolution 748 (VIII) of 27 November 1953.
[25] General Assembly resolution 849 (IX) of 22 November 1954.
[26] General Assembly resolution 945 (X) of 15 December 1955.
[27] General Assembly resolution 1469 (XIV) of 12 December 1959.

been approved by previously elected legislatures, and not by referenda, or elections called exclusively to pass on the new proposals; that the United Kingdom had opposed any visit by the United Nations; that the United Nations had been presented with a *fait accompli*, and had not been involved in the process of ascertaining the true wishes of the population; and that the people had been given no alternatives. Therefore, it was the feeling of the majority that the decolonization process of these territories had not been completed, and that the situation in these territories needed further United Nations scrutiny, preferably *in situ*. It is quite possible that if a procedure similar to that used for the Cook Islands had been followed, the choice of the people would not have been different.

PART I—GENERAL CONSIDERATIONS

CHAPTER ONE

DEFINITION, SCOPE AND BASIC DATA

What is a "very small state or territory," a "micro-state," a "mini-territory?"[1] These terms have never been defined adequately. The Secretary-General, in the Introduction to his Annual Report 1966-67, refers to "entities which are exceptionally small in area, population and human and economic resources."[2]

If smallness or size *per se* is to become a factor in the establishment of criteria for admission to the United Nations, or an element in the determination of a country's ability to carry out the obligations contained in the Charter, then a definition—simple or complex—may have to be worked out. On the other hand, if one is interested in the general aspects and consequences of smallness, and in new forms of United Nations assistance to small states and territories, then there is no real need for a rigorous definition. In that case, various elements of smallness ought to be taken into account, and, as a result, certain small states and territories may be considered, generally or only from certain points of view, as belonging to a special group in which the consequences of smallness are of particular importance.

In a paper prepared for the seminar organized in 1962-64 by the Institute of Commonwealth Studies, one of the authors stated that "it proved impossible to decide what 'smallness' means with any precision. It is a comparative and not an absolute idea. Whatever scales of magnitude are employed seem arbitrary, and it is difficult to pick out of them where smallness begins or ends. Countries can be small in one sense and not in another. Smallness in whatever form it may exist is only one of the variables. The issue is complicated still further by the significant

---

[1] Mini- or micro-state is used here for a very small independent state, mini-territory for a very small dependent territory.

[2] A/6701/Add.1, para. 163.

factor of remoteness, whether simple geographical remoteness of remoteness from the intellectual mainstreams of the world."[3]

The World Data Analysis Program of Yale University was asked to look into the question of the possible criteria of the concept mini-state or mini-territory, and the standing of that concept in terms of theoretical political science. An Annex to this study contains the analysis made for UNITAR by Professor Taylor, of the Data Analysis Program of Yale University, with the use of several variables such as population, area, GNP, energy consumption, legal status, political self-perception, distances, etc., and the use of techniques such as hierarchical clustering and analysis of variance.

The conclusion is that there are many ways to define a mini-state or mini-territory, but they are all more or less arbitrary. The use of a single variable is too narrow a conception.

If the states and territories of the world are distributed along the size scales of area, population and GNP, any cut-off point for "micro" is arbitrary. However, the study shows that it is possible with these three variables to group the states and territories rationally by separating those which show more similarity to each other in respect to their position along all the three scales taken together. It shows also that other factors may be taken into consideration, for example, "isolation."

The present chapter will be limited to giving the reader a few factual data bearing on smallness, without going any further into the question of definition.

First of all, it should be noted that this study is interested exclusively in states and territories which have already or still had recently *some degree of international individuality*, however tenuous, and not in those which do not have or do not claim any degree of international separateness. There are, however, borderline cases, or cases where the international character which has been non-existent so far suddenly comes to the fore, so that even from that point of view there is an element of arbitrariness and uncertainty which should be kept in mind when looking at any list of small states and territories.[4]

Table I gives such a list of most small states and territories with a population of 1,000,000 or less, without going into the question as to which of these constitute "real" mini-states or mini-territories. The grouping is by geographical area, with a distinction made between mainland territories (39) and islands or groups of islands (57).

Table Ia shows the approximate number of islands in each island group.

[3] *Problems of Smaller Territories,* edited by Burton Benedict, University of London, 1967, p. 29.
[4] The inclusion or exclusion of small territories in Tables I to VII will be better understood by referring to Table VII (classification according to status).

In the determination of smallness, an essential element is *population*. But what level should the population reach to justify that the territory is no longer in the "very small" category? Any unqualified answer would be quite arbitrary. Factual information is contained in Table II, listing the 96 states and territories included in Table I by population. The upper limit population figure of one million has been arbitrarily chosen, without attaching any magic value to it.

Table III gives the same list of 96 territories according to *area*. As a matter of interest, this list also gives the area and population of Hong Kong and Singapore, two city-territories small as far as area is concerned but with fairly large populations, way over one million.

For any territory, large or small, the notion of area has a different value according to whether or not it includes huge proportions of desert, of uninhabitable or unproductive land; for small territories, special consideration should also be given to the lack of comparability between mainland areas, island areas and groups of island areas: Luxembourg (2,586 sq. km.) is a "one-piece" country surrounded by other lands; Réunion (2,510 sq. km.) is one island surrounded by water; the Trust Territory of the Pacific Islands (1,779 sq. km.) is a territory composed of some 2,100 islands (of which only 96 are inhabited) which are scattered over an ocean area of 7,700,000 sq. km. The similarity of land area of these three territories is therefore only superficial, and any comparison has to be qualified.

Table IV gives the *density of population* by territory, based on Tables II and III.

One should be cautious in making comparisons and assessing the meaning of the density of the population of a large island (Cyprus: density 65) and that of a group of 2,100 small islands (Trust Territory of the Pacific Islands: density 52). Within the component parts of a territory, density may vary considerably, and the average may be less meaningful. (Southern Yemen: 3.9 population per sq. km.; component parts: former State of Aden—1,288 per sq. km.; former Federation of South Arabia—14 per sq. km.; former Western Protectorate—9.8 per sq. km.; former Eastern Protectorate—1.4 per sq. km.)

TABLE I—SMALL STATES AND TERRITORIES BY GEOGRAPHICAL AREA
A. Mainland[a]

Africa	America	Asia	Oceania	Europe	Near East
Botswana	British Honduras	Bhutan	Papua [New Guinea]	Andorra	Bahrein
Cabinda	French Guiana	Brunei	West Irian	Gibraltar	Kuwait
Congo (Brazzaville)	Guyana	Macao		Holy See	Muscat and Oman
Equatorial Guinea	Panama Canal Zone	Sabah		Liechtenstein	Qatar
	Surinam	Sarawak		Luxembourg	Trucial States
French Territory of the Afars and Issas		Sikkim		Monaco	
Gabon				San Marino	
The Gambia					
Portuguese Guinea					
Ifni					
Lesotho					
Spanish Sahara					
South-West Africa (Namibia)					
Swaziland					
Western Cameroons					

[a] Including parts of very large islands (Sabah, Sarawak, Papua, West Irian), or areas adjacent to the mainland (Bahrein).

B. Islands or groups of islands

Atlantic Ocean	Caribbean	Mediterranean	Indian Ocean	Pacific Ocean
Bermuda	Antigua	Cyprus	British Indian	American Samoa
Cape Verde Islands	Bahamas	Malta	Ocean Territory	Cook Islands
Channel Islands	Barbados		Cocos (Keeling)	Fiji
Falkland Islands	Cayman Islands		Islands	French Polynesia
Faroe Islands	Dominica		Comoro	Gilbert and Ellice
Iceland	Grenada		Archipelago	Islands
Isle of Man	Gaudeloupe		Christmas Island	Guam
St. Helena (with Ascension	Martinique		Maldive Islands	Nauru
and Tristan da Cunha)	Montserrat		Mauritius	New Caledonia
St. Pierre-et-Miquelon	Netherlands		Réunion	New Hebrides
Sao Tomé and Principe	Antilles		Seychelles	Niue
[Fernando Poo: see	St. Kitts-Nevis-			Norfolk Island
Afrique: Equatorial	Anguilla			Pitcairn Island
Guinea]	St. Lucia			Ryukyu
	St. Vincent			Solomon Islands
	Trinidad and			Timor
	Tobago			Tokelau
	Turks and Caicos			Tonga
	Islands			Trust Territory of
	British Virgin			the Pacific
	Islands			Islands
	U.S. Virgin			Wallis and Futuna
	Islands			Western Samoa

TABLE Ia—SMALL STATES AND TERRITORIES
Islands or groups of islands

The information given in this Table about the approximate number of islands in each group and how many are inhabited is neither accurate nor reliable. The data on which these figures are based are incomplete and contain conflicting information. This is not surprising, as there seems to be no standard practice of the extent to which islets, cays and even rocks should be included in the count of islands. Information on inhabited islands is also incomplete and to a large degree inaccurate. The Table below is therefore subject to correction. Its main aim is to indicate how greatly the situation varies from one case to another.

	Approx. number of islands	Approx. number of inhabited islands	Total land area (sq. km.)	Estimated population
(a) *Islands in the Atlantic Ocean*				
Bermuda	300	20	53	50,000
Cape Verde Islands	14	10	4,033	228,000
Channel Islands	16	11	195	115,000
Falkland Islands	200	12	11,961	2,000
Faroe Islands	21	17	1,399	37,000
Iceland	1	1	103,000	195,000
Isle of Man	1	1	588	50,000
St. Helena, Ascension, Tristan da Cunha	3	3	314	5,815
St. Pierre-et-Miquelon	8	2	242	5,000
Sao Tomé and Principe	[2	2	964	59,000]
[Fernando Poo: part of Equatorial Guinea]	[2	2	2,034	74,000]
(b) *Islands in the Caribbean*				
Antigua	3	2	442	60,000
Bahamas	700	30	11,406	140,000
Barbados	1	1	430	245,000
Cayman Islands	3	3	259	9,000
Dominica	1	1	751	68,000
Grenada	2	2	344	97,000
Guadeloupe	7	7	1,779	319,000
Martinique	1	1	1,102	327,000
Montserrat	1	1	98	14,000
Netherlands Antilles	6	6	961	210,000
St. Kitts-Nevis-Anguilla	4	4	357	61,000
St. Lucia	1	1	616	103,000
St. Vincent	6	6	388	90,000
Trinidad and Tobago	3	3	5,128	1,000,000

TABLE Ia—(continued)

	Ap-prox. number of islands	Ap-prox. number of in-habited islands	Total land area (sq. km.)	Esti-mated popu-lation
Turks and Caicos	30	6	430	6,000
British Virgin Islands	40	11	153	9,000
U.S. Virgin Islands	50	3	344	50,000
(c) *Islands in the Mediterranean Sea*				
Cyprus	1	1	9,251	603,000
Malta	5	3	316	317,000
(d) *Islands in the Indian Ocean*				
British Indian Ocean Territory	25	?	74	2,000
Cocos (Keeling) Islands	27	3	14	1,000
Comoros	7	4	2,171	225,000
Christmas Island	1	1	135	3,000
Maldive Islands	2,000	220	298	101,000
Mauritius	4	4	2,096	780,000
Réunion	1	1	2,510	408,000
Seychelles	89	4	404	49,000
(e) *Islands in the Pacific Ocean*				
American Samoa	7	6	197	27,000
Cook Islands	15	14	234	21,000
Fiji	300	100	18,160	478,000
French Polynesia[a]	125	100	4,000	90,000
Gilbert and Ellice Islands[b]	37	31	886	54,000
Guam	1	1	549	79,000
Nauru	1	1	21	6,000
New Caledonia	40	5	19,000	93,000
New Hebrides	80	30	14,763	70,000
Niue	1	1	259	5,000
Norfolk Island	1	1	36	1,000
Pitcairn	4	1	5	92
Ryukyu and Bonin	100	90	2,196	944,000
Solomon Islands (Br.)	100	90	29,785	140,000
Timor	4	4	18,990	560,000
Tokelau	3	3	10	2,000
Tonga	200	40	699	75,000
Trust Territory of the Pacific Islands[c]	2,100	96	1,770	94,000
Wallis and Futuna	25	3	200	8,000
Western Samoa	8	8	2,842	130,000

[a] Ocean area: 4 million sq. km.
[b] Ocean area: 5 million sq. km.
[c] Ocean area: 7 million sq. km.

TABLE II—SMALL STATES AND TERRITORIES WITH A POPULATION OF ONE MILLION OR LESS[a]

Classification by population

	Population (UN mid-1966 estimates)		Area (Square kilometres)	
1. Trinidad and Tobago	1,000,000		5,128	
2. Ryukyu	944,000		2,196	
3. Lesotho	865,000		30,344	
4. Sarawak	862,000		125,205	
5. Congo (Brazzaville)	850,000		342,000	
6. Western Cameroons	826,000		43,000	
7. West Irian	800,000		412,781	
8. Mauritius	780,000		2,096	
9. Bhutan	750,000		47,000	
10. Guyana	662,000		214,970	
11. Cyprus	603,000		9,251	
12. Papua[b]	601,000		222,998	
13. South-West Africa (Namibia)	584,000		824,292	
14. Botswana	580,000		569,581	
15. Muscat and Oman	565,000		212,379	
16. Timor	560,000		18,990	
17. Sabah	551,000		76,115	
18. Portuguese Guinea	529,000		36,125	
19. Kuwait	491,000		16,000	
20. Fiji	478,000		18,169	
21. Gabon	468,000		267,667	
22. Réunion	408,000		2,510	
23. Swaziland	390,000		17,363	
24. Surinam	345,000		142,822	
25. The Gambia	336,000		11,295	
26. Luxembourg	335,000		2,586	
27. Martinique	327,000		1,102	
28. Guadeloupe	319,000		1,779	
29. Malta	317,000		316	
30. Equatorial Guinea	272,000		28,051	
(Rio Muni		198,000		26,017
(Fernando Poo		74,000		2,034
31. Macao	250,000		16	
32. Barbados	245,000		430	
33. Cape Verde Islands	228,000		4,033	
34. Comoro Archipelago	225,000		2,171	
35. Netherlands Antilles	210,000		961	
36. Iceland	195,000		103,000	

[a] See also Table VII. Examples given in this table are not intended to show the legal or constitutional status of these entities.
[b] Administered jointly with the Trust Territory of New Guinea. The combined Territory of Papua-New Guinea has a population of 2,183,000 and an area of 461,691 sq. km.

TABLE II—(continued)

	Population (UN mid-1966 estimates)	Area (square kilometres)
37. Bahrein	193,000	598
38. Sikkim	180,000	7,107
39. Solomon Islands	140,000	29,785
40. Bahamas	140,000	11,406
41. Trucial States	130,000	83,600
42. Western Samoa	130,000	2,930
43. French Territory of the Afars and Issas	125,000	22,000
44. Channel Islands	115,000	195
45. British Honduras	109,000	22,563
46. Brunei	104,000	5,765
47. St. Lucia	103,000	616
48. Maldive Islands	101,000	298
49. Grenada	97,000	344
50. Trust Territory of the Pacific Islands	94,000	1,779
51. New Caledonia	93,000	19,000
52. St. Vincent	90,000	388
53. French Polynesia	90,000	4,000
54. Guam	79,000	549
55. Tonga	75,000	700
56. Qatar	71,000	22,014
57. New Hebrides	70,000	14,763
58. Dominica	68,000	751
59. St. Kitts-Nevis-Anguilla	61,000	357
60. Cabinda	60,000	7,270
61. Antigua	60,000	442
62. Sao Tomé and Principe	59,000	964
63. Panama Canal Zone	56,000	1,432
64. Gilbert and Ellice Islands	54,000	886
65. Ifni	53,000	1,500
66. Bermuda	50,000	53
67. U.S. Virgin Islands	50,000	344
68. Isle of Man	50,000	588
69. Seychelles	49,000	404
70. Spanish Sahara	48,000	266,000
71. French Guiana	37,000	90,000
72. Faroe Islands	37,000	1,399
73. American Samoa	27,000	197
74. Gibraltar	25,000	6
75. Monaco	23,000	1.5
76. Cook Islands	21,000	234
77. Liechtenstein	19,000	157
78. San Marino	18,000	61

TABLE II—(continued)

	Population (UN mid-1966 estimates)	Area (square kilometres)
79. Montserrat	14,000	98
80. Andorra	11,000	453
81. Cayman Islands	9,000	259
82. British Virgin Islands	9,000	153
83. Wallis and Futuna	8,000	200
84. Turks and Caicos Islands	6,000	430
85. Nauru	6,000	21
86. St. Helena, Ascension, Tristan da Cunha	5,815	314
(St. Helena	5,000	122
(Ascension	530	88
(Tristan da Cunha	285	104
87. Niue	5,000	259
88. St. Pierre-et-Miquelon	5,000	242
89. Christmas Island	3,000	145
90. Falkland Islands	2,000	11,961
91. British Indian Ocean Territory	2,000	74
92. Tokelau	2,000	10
93. Cocos (Keeling) Islands	1,000	14
94. Holy See	1,000	0.44
95. Norfolk Island	1,000	36
96. Pitcairn Island	92	5
	22,095,907	

Recapitulation

900,001–1,000,000:	2		90,001–100,000:	3
800,001– 900,000:	5		80,001– 90,000:	2
700,001– 800,000:	2		70,001– 80,000:	3
600,001– 700,000:	3		60,001– 70,000:	3
500,001– 600,000:	6		50,001– 60,000:	6
400,001– 500,000:	4		40,001– 50,000:	5
300,001– 400,000:	7		30,001– 40,000:	2
200,001– 300,000:	6		20,001– 30,000:	4
100,001– 200,000:	13		10,001– 20,000:	4
			1– 10,000:	16
	48			48

TABLE III—SMALL STATES AND TERRITORIES

Classification by area

(1 sq. mile = 2.59 sq. km.
1 sq. km. = 0.38 sq. mile)

	Area (square kilometres)	Population (UN mid-1966 estimates)
1. South-West Africa (Namibia)	824,292	584,000
2. Botswana	569,581	580,000
3. West Irian	412,781	800,000
4. Congo (Brazzaville)	342,000	850,000
5. Gabon	267,667	468,000
6. Spanish Sahara	266,000	48,000
7. Papua	222,998	601,000
8. Guyana	214,969	662,000
9. Muscat and Oman	212,379	565,000
10. Surinam	142,822	345,000
11. Sarawak	125,205	862,000
12. Iceland	103,000	195,000
13. French Guiana	91,000	37,000
14. Trucial States	83,600	130,000
15. Sabah	76,115	551,000
16. Bhutan	47,000	750,000
17. Western Cameroons	43,000	826,000
18. Portuguese Guinea	36,125	529,000
19. Lesotho	30,344	865,000
20. Solomon Islands	29,785	140,000
21. Equatorial Guinea	28,051	272,000
(Rio Muni	26,017	198,000
(Fernando Poo	2,034	74,000
22. British Honduras	22,965	109,000
23. Qatar	22,014	71,000
24. French Territory of the Afars and Issas	22,000	125,000
25. New Caledonia	19,000	93,000
26. Timor	18,990	560,000
27. Fiji	18,169	478,000
28. Swaziland	17,360	390,000
29. Kuwait	16,000	491,000
30. New Hebrides	14,763	70,000
31. Falkland Islands	11,961	2,000
32. Bahamas	11,406	140,000
33. The Gambia	11,295	336,000
34. Cyprus	9,251	603,000
35. Cabinda	7,270	60,000
36. Sikkim	7,107	180,000
37. Brunei	5,765	104,000

TABLE III—(continued)

	Area (square kilometres)	Population (UN mid-1966 estimates)	
38. Trinidad and Tobago	5,128	1,000,000	
39. Cape Verde Islands	4,033	228,000	
40. French Polynesia	4,000	90,000	
41. Western Samoa	2,842	130,000	
42. Luxembourg	2,586	335,000	
43. Réunion	2,510	408,000	
44. Ryukyu	2,196	944,000	
45. Comoro Archipelago	2,171	225,000	
46. Mauritius	2,096	780,000	
47. Trust Territory of the Pacific Islands	1,779	94,000	
48. Guadeloupe	1,779	319,000	
49. Ifni	1,500	53,000	
50. Panama Canal Zone	1,432	56,000	
51. Faroe Islands	1,399	37,000	
52. Martinique	1,102	327,000	
53. Sao Tomé and Principe	964	59,000	
54. Netherlands Antilles	961	210,000	
55. Gilbert and Ellice Islands	886	54,000	
56. Dominica	751	68,000	
57. Tonga	699	75,000	
58. St. Lucia	616	103,000	
59. Bahrein	598	193,000	
60. Isle of Man	588	50,000	
61. Guam	549	79,000	
62. Andorra	465	11,000	
63. Antigua	442	60,000	
64. Barbados	430	245,000	
65. Turks and Caicos Islands	430	6,000	
66. Seychelles	404	49,000	
67. St. Vincent	388	90,000	
68. St. Kitts-Nevis-Anguilla	357	61,000	
69. Grenada	344	97,000	
70. U.S. Virgin Islands	344	50,000	
71. Malta	316	317,000	
72. St. Helena, Ascension and Tristan da Cunha	314	5,815	
(St. Helena	122		5,000
(Ascension	88		530
(Tristan da Cunha	104		285
73. Maldive Islands	298	101,000	
74. Cayman Islands	259	9,000	
75. Niue	259	5,000	
76. St. Pierre-et-Miquelon	242	5,000	

TABLE III—(continued)

	Area (square kilometres)	Population (UN mid-1966 estimates)
77. Cook Islands	234	21,000
78. Wallis and Futuna	200	8,000
79. American Samoa	197	27,000
80. Channel Islands	195	115,000
81. Liechtenstein	157	19,000
82, British Virgin Islands	153	9,000
83. Christmas Island	135	3,000
84. Montserrat	98	14,000
85. British Indian Ocean Territory	74	2,000
86. San Marino	61	18,000
87. Bermuda	53	50,000
88. Norfolk Island	36	1,000
89. Nauru	21	6,000
90. Macao	16	250,000
91. Cocos (Keeling) Islands	14	1,000
92. Tokelau	10	2,000
93. Gibraltar	6	25,000
94. Pitcairn Island	5	92
95. Monaco	1.5	23,000
96. Holy See	0.44	1,000
[Hong Kong	1,031	3,716,000
Singapore	581	1,914,000]

TABLE IV—SMALL STATES AND TERRITORIES

Density of Population

	Population per sq. km.		Population per sq. km.
1. Macao	15,625	13. Martinique	296
2. Monaco	15,333	14. San Marino	295
3. Gibraltar	4,166	15. Nauru	285
4. Holy See	2,272	16. Grenada	281
5. Malta	1,003	17. St. Vincent	231
6. Bermuda	943	18. Netherlands Antilles	218
7. Channel Islands	589	19. Tokelau Islands	200
8. Barbados	569	20. Trinidad and Tobago	195
9. Mauritius	437	21. Guadeloupe	179
10. Ryukyu	429	22. St. Kitts-Nevis-	
11. Maldive Islands	338	Anguilla	170
12. Bahrein	322	23. St. Lucia	167

TABLE IV—(continued)

	Population per sq. km.		Population per sq. km.
24. Réunion	162	62. St. Pierre-et-Miquelon	20
25. U.S. Virgin Islands	145	63. Christmas Island	20
26. Guam	143	64. Niue	19
27. Montserrat	142	65. Western Cameroons	19
28. American Samoa	137	66. St. Helena, Ascension, Tristan da Cunha	18
29. Antigua	135		
30. Luxembourg	129		
31. Seychelles	121	67. Pitcairn Island	18
32. Liechtenstein	121	68. Brunei	18
33. Tonga	107	69. Bhutan	15
34. Comoro Archipelago	103	70. Portuguese Guinea	14
35. Dominica	90	71. Turks and Caicos Islands	13
36. Cook Islands	89		
37. Isle of Man	85	72. Bahamas	12
38. Cocos (Keeling) Islands	71	73. Equatorial Guinea	9.6
		74. Cabinda	8.2
39. Cyprus	65	75. Sabah	7.2
40. Sao Tomé and Principe	61	76. Sarawak	6.8
41. Gilbert and Ellice Islands	60	77. French Territory of the Afars and Issas	5.6
42. British Virgin Islands	58	78. British Honduras	4.8
		79. New Caledonia	4.8
43. Cape Verde Islands	56	80. Solomon Islands	4.7
44. Trust Territory of the Pacific Islands	52	81. New Hebrides	4.7
		82. Qatar	3.2
45. Western Samoa	44	83. Guyana	3.0
46. Wallis and Futuna	40	84. Papua	2.6
47. Panama Canal Zone	39	85. Muscat and Oman	2.6
48. Ifni	35	86. Congo (Brazzaville)	2.4
49. Cayman Islands	34	87. Surinam	2.4
50. Kuwait	30	88. West Irian	1.9
51. The Gambia	29	89. Iceland	1.9
52. Timor	29	90. Gabon	1.7
53. Lesotho	28	91. Trucial States	1.5
54. Norfolk Island	27	92. Botswana	1.0
55. British Indian Ocean Territory	27	93. South-West Africa (Namibia)	0.7
56. Faroe Islands	26	94. French Guiana	0.4
57. Fiji	26	95. Spanish Sahara	0.2
58. Sikkim	25	96. Falkland Islands	0.2
59. Andorra	24	[Hong Kong	3,604
60. French Polynesia	22	Singapore	3,295]
61. Swaziland	22		

A classification of small states and territories based on legal status is given in a subsequent chapter.[5] Economic indicators for selected territories are also contained in a further chapter.[6] But the data given above on population, size, density of population, dispersion on the oceans are already sufficient to indicate how diverse these territories are, how conditions vary and how cautious one has to be before making any generalization about them.

A superficial look at some available political, economic and social indicators shows what an uneven lot the mini-states and mini-territories are.

Some small states seem to be healthy, happy and even prosperous little pieces of real estate, and in many respects they compare favourably with much larger states: Luxembourg and Kuwait, for example. Many others are in a less favourable position. Many have so few resources that they have apparently no future if they remain isolated: the Cook Islands, for example. Others, however, Malta, Barbados, Western Samoa, for example, while they are by no means in a very enviable position, are nevertheless doing better in certain fields than larger countries, where the lack of resources and of capital, the outlook for development and the population pressure are comparatively more frightening.

It is difficult to evaluate these situations in precise, objective and quantitative terms, in order to avoid the use of impressionistic value judgments about the "viability" or "non-viability" of small territories.

A cursory examination has been made of the data included in the *World Handbook of Political and Social Indicators*, by Russett, Alker, Deutsch and Lasswell, published by Yale University Press in 1964. Out of the 75 tables, 17 cover from 104 to 133 countries and territories, among which are included 12 to 16 relatively small territories[7] (four between 1-3 million: Hong Kong, Puerto Rico, Singapore, Aden; five between 0.5 and 1 million: Trinidad and Tobago, Sarawak, Mauritius, British Guiana, Cyprus; seven between 0.1 and 0.5 million: Malta, Kuwait, Surinam, Luxembourg, Barbados, Netherlands Antilles, Iceland; none below 0.1 million). These tables relate to the following subjects:

TABLE 1 —Total population 1961 (in 1,000)
TABLE 40—Area (in sq. km.)

[5] See Table VII.
[6] See Part III, Chapter One.
[7] The territories are referred to in the Handbook as they existed at the time the statistical data were gathered. In the meantime, changes have occurred: Aden, Singapore, Trinidad and Tobago, Guyana, Cyprus, Malta, Kuwait, Barbados have since become independent, and Sarawak is now part of the Federation of Malaysia. The figures given for Aden relate to the Territory of the former Federation of South Arabia, which is part of what is now the independent state of Southern Yemen.

TABLE 41—Population per sq. km.
TABLE 9 —% of population in cities over 20,000
TABLE 2 —% of population of working age
TABLE 8 —Annual % rate of increase in population (1958–1961)
TABLE 31—Daily newspaper circulation per 1,000 population
TABLE 35—Radios per 1,000 population
TABLE 38—Cinema attendance per capita
TABLE 42—Population per 1,000 hectares of agricultural land
TABLE 43—GNP 1957 $US ($ million)
TABLE 44—GNP per capita 1957 ($US)
TABLE 59—Inhabitants per physician
TABLE 60—Inhabitants per hospital bed
TABLE 62—Students enrolled in higher education per 100,000
        population
TABLE 63—Primary and secondary pupils as % population aged
        5–19
TABLE 64—% literate of population aged 15 and over.

Absolute figures for the sixteen territories are given in Table V, below. Table VI gives the rank of these territories for each table. In most cases (except obviously total population, area and total GNP), they are spread above and below the mean and median ranks, often in the middle of the range. In other words, for most of these indicators, they rank neither at the top nor at the bottom of the list.

The number of territories included in these tables is obviously inadequate, and the choice may not be representative. For example, there are no samples of the smaller mini-territories (under 100,000). Also, the variables chosen may not be the most significant ones, and the basis of the statistical data may in some cases be shaky. The comparison is, however, interesting, and if more mini-territories could be covered, and more variables included, comparison with bigger states and correlations between variables might be of greater interest. Extreme caution would still be necessary in reaching any conclusions about the relative standing of mini-states (one should, in particular, be very careful in the interpretation given and the importance attached to GNP *per capita*). The main difficulty is the lack of reliable statistical data about many of the small territories.

TABLE V—STATISTICAL DATA ON SELECTED SMALL STATES AND TERRITORIES

(Extracted from the *World Handbook of Political and Social Indicators*, by Bruce M. Russett and others—Yale University Press, 1964)

FIGURES	TABLE 1 Total population 1961 in 1,000	TABLE 40 Area sq. km.	TABLE 41 Population per sq. km.	TABLE 9 % of population in cities over 20,000	TABLE 2 % of population of working age	TABLE 8 Annual % rate of increase in population 1958–1961	TABLE 31 Daily newspaper circulation per 1,000 population	TABLE 35 Radios per 1,000 population
No. of cases	133	133	133	120	128	111	125	118
% World population	99	99	99	98	98	97	98	74
Mean	22,864	979,754	144	23.1	57.8	2.3	102.1	111.2
Median	5,496	245,857	27	18.3	56.6	2.2	54	65.4
Hong Kong	3,178	1,013	3,081	81.9	54.9	3.6	223	55.3
Puerto Rico	2,409	8,897	271	32	52.1	1.6	61	—
Singapore	1,687	581	2,904	—	55	3.7	140	88.3
Aden	1,210	290,374	4	—	64.1	—	—	49.6
Trinidad and Tobago	859	5,128	168	75.1	54.1	2.9	86	84.1
Sarawak	760	123,025	6	7	52.5	5.1	25	55.3
Mauritius	656	2,096	352	27.4	52.8	2.8	89	—
British Guiana	582	214,970	3	17.9	52.1	3	79	72.2
Cyprus	577	9,251	62	13.6	58.6	1.1	123	178
Malta and Gozo	329	316	1,041	7.3	56.1	0.7	124	222
Kuwait	322	15,540	21	50.6	61.8	15.1	4	—
Surinam	321	142,822	2	72.4	51.1	4.5	67	129.9
Luxembourg	317	2,586	123	30.3	70	0.7	445	319
Barbados	236	431	548	54.7	60.2	—	85	161
Netherlands Antilles	194	961	202	—	—	1.2	129	207.5
Iceland	179	103,000	2	40.5	57.1	2	450	279

TABLE V—(Continued)

	TABLE 38	TABLE 42	TABLE 43	TABLE 44	TABLE 59	TABLE 60	TABLE 62	TABLE 63	TABLE 64
	Cinema attend-ance per capita	Popu-lation per 1,000 hectares of agri-cultural land	GNP 1957 $U.S. ($ million)	GNP per capita 1957 $U.S.	Inhab-itants per physician	Inhab-itants per hospital bed	Students enrolled in higher education per 100,000 popu-lation	Primary and secondary pupils as % popula-tion aged 5-19	% literate of popu-lation aged 15 and over
	104	115	122	122	126	129	105	125	118
	94	96	99	99	98	98	97	98	97
	6.27	2,941	9,453	377	1,508	789	281	43	52.1
	4.7	1,103	1,063	191.5	3,750	330	220	46	50
	22.8	98,143	640	272	3,300	390	176	49	57.5
	3.4	4,030	1,286	563	2,200	190	1,192	66	81
	13.8	108,214	584	400	2,400	300	437	63	50
	1.1	—	95	120	11,200	1,400	—	—	5
	9	4,383	324	423	2,300	210	61	64	73.8
	15.7	86	64	100	15,000	600	—	40	21
	11.4	4,711	150	225	4,500	210	14	64	51.8
	7.7	192	121	235	3,900	200	27	68	74
	8.5	1,042	250	467	1,400	210	78	55	60.5
	13.1	8,050	120	377	980	110	142	82	57.6
	0.9	55	603	2,900	930	120	—	47	30
	5.4	—	33	142	2,000	190	109	64	72.5
	14.3	2,286	439	1,388	910	90	36	52	96.5
	7.8	7,121	46	200	3,000	180	24	70	91.1
	8.8	33,400	30	160	1,400	110	—	57	—
	—	79	94	572	840	100	445	89	98.5

TABLE VI—RANK OF SELECTED SMALL STATES AND TERRITORIES

Key: — = above mean, and below median
     [ ] = below mean, and above median

RANKS	TABLE 1 Total population 1961	TABLE 40 Area	TABLE 41 Population per sq. km.	TABLE 9 % of population in cities over 20,000	TABLE 2 % of population of working age	TABLE 8 Annual % rate of increase in population 1958–1961	TABLE 31 Daily newspaper circulation per 1,000 population	TABLE 35 Radios per 1,000 population
No. of cases	133	133	133	120	128	111	125	118
% of World population	99	99	99	98	98	97	98	74
Mean (rank)	21.5	29.5	20.5	49.5	55	49	39.5	39.5
Median (rank)	67	67	66	60.5	64.5	54	69	59.5
Hong Kong	84	129	1	1	90	11	22	67.5
Puerto Rico	96	125	9	33.5	116.5	80.5	59.5	—
Singapore	106	131	2	—	89	8.5	31	47
Aden	115	60	114.5	—	20.5	—	—	73
Trinidad and Tobago	119	126	16	2	100	30	45	49
Sarawak	120	89	109.5	96	109	2	74.5	67.5
Mauritius	122	128	5	43	107	33.5	44	53
British Guiana	123	73	119	63	116.5	25.5	49	
Cyprus	124	124	49	74	48.5	87.5		15
Malta and Gozo	127	133	3	95	66.5	102	37	30
Kuwait	128	121	71.5	11	33		36	21
Surinam	129	82	125	3		1	107	38
Luxembourg	130	127	25	37	122	4	53.5	65
Barbados	131	132	4	9	1	102	5	34
Netherlands Antilles	132	130	14	—	37.5	—	46	23
Iceland	133	97	125	19	60	65	4	15

TABLE VI—(Continued)

TABLE 38	TABLE 42	TABLE 43	TABLE 44	TABLE 59	TABLE 60	TABLE 62	TABLE 63	TABLE 64
Cinema attendance per capita	Population per 1,000 hectares of agricultural land	GNP 1957	GNP per capita 1957	Inhabitants per physician	Inhabitants per hospital bed	Students enrolled in higher education per 100,000 population	Primary and secondary pupils as % of population aged 5-19	% literate of population aged 15 and over
104	115	122	122	126	129	105	125	118
94	96	99	99	98	98	97	98	97
47	21.5	18.5	37	88	35	40.5	63	59
52	58	61.5	61.5	63.5	66	53	62	61.5
1	2	76	4.9	[66]	62	57	57.5	54.5
62	16	56	24	[78]	90.5	2	24	32
12.5	1	79	34	[75]	72.5	24	29.5	61.5
82.5	—	111	83	35	19	—	—	109
29	15	95.5	33	[77]	84	78	27	43
7	107	116	89	31	45	—	66.5	84
20	14	106	55	58.5	84	94.5	27	60
37	95	108	54	61.5	87	89	21.5	42
34	60	101	31	89.5	84	71.5	45	50
16	7	109	37	100	114.5	63	2	53
85	110	77	1	103.5	108	—	59.5	77
50	—	121	77	[81.5]	90.5	67	27	44
10	29	86	5	105	124	85	51.5	21
36	9	120	60	[68]	94.5	90	17	26
36	3	122	72.5	89.5	114.5	—	39.5	—
—	108	112.5	23	110	119.5	23	1	7.5

CHAPTER TWO

FACTORS EXPLAINING WHY VERY SMALL TERRITORIES EXIST OR HAVE EXISTED AS SEPARATE INTERNATIONAL ENTITIES RATHER THAN AS INTERNATIONALLY UNDISTINGUISHABLE COMPONENTS OF LARGER POLITICAL UNITS

Regardless of whether a small territorial unit is physically or legally qualified to become an independent state, why does it have—or claim to have—a separate international personality?

Some of the causes are obvious. Others are less easy to ascertain.

The most obvious factor is physical, geographical isolation. This element is particularly strong in the case of islands, especially remote ones. Typical examples include Nauru, Samoa, Fiji in the Pacific; Bermuda, Barbados, the Leeward and Windward Islands in the Caribbean; the Maldive Islands in the Indian Ocean; St. Helena, Ascension, Tristan da Cunha in the Atlantic; Malta in the Mediterranean, etc. But physical isolation is not exclusively of the insular type: consider landlocked Andorra, almost entirely surrounded by high mountains, or Sikkim.

Insularity and distance can have a divisive effect even within a group of islands having a common political status: the Federation of the West Indies did not succeed in keeping the British islands of the Caribbean together; in the Trust Territory of the Pacific Islands, centrifugal forces are at work among the Marshalls, Carolines and Marianas.

Other factors can be found in historical developments, particularly in accidents of colonization. It is in studying history that one can discover why Andorra, Monaco, San Marino, Gibraltar, etc., are now distinct from their neighbours. Accidental developments in the colonial scramble for Africa explain the emergence of The Gambia, French Somaliland, Lesotho, etc., as small distinct units in the African picture.

Such historical accidents may combine with geographical isolation further to complicate the picture: if the separate existence of the Samoan Islands is due to geographical isolation, the fact that Western Samoa and American Samoa are each going their separate way is due to freakish developments of colonialism and big power competition.

Geographical and historical situations may be reinforced by pre-existent factors of differentiation such as language, religion, race, etc. For example, the fact that certain islands of the Pacific were inhabited by psychologically self-centred Polynesians has certainly contributed to the preservation of the individuality of these islands. But more often it has worked in reverse. Because of historical accidents, new factors of differentiation have developed which prevent a given area from re-establishing normal links with its neighbours, once the previous accidental barriers are removed. The occupation of The Gambia by the British has resulted in the widespread use of the English language, deeply ingrained institutions on the British model, educational, intellectual and sentimental links with England, a pattern of trade with the Sterling area, all of which prevented closer integration with surrounding French-speaking and French-oriented Senegal when the entire area broke loose from British and French colonial domination. Many other examples can be given on the effects of imported languages, religions, political, social and economic patterns which have resulted in crystallizing the separateness of a small territory at a time when the original reason for its differentiation in the area no longer existed.

Competing claims may also be instrumental in developing or preserving a distinct territorial identity. As is well known, Ethiopia and Somalia have conflicting views about French Somaliland (presently named French Territory of the Afars and Issas). Likewise, pressure from Morocco and Mauritania may have a bearing on the existence of Spanish Sahara.

The opinion of a single big neighbour may also help determine the continued separate existence of the adjacent mini-territory. India claimed that the French establishments in India and Portuguese Goa were integral parts of India. As a result, with the co-operation of France and against the will of Portugal, these territories were integrated with India. China claims that Hong Kong and Macao are integral parts of China; however, these territories remain at present under British and Portuguese administration. The separate status of Lesotho, Botswana and Swaziland is now accepted by their neighbour, South Africa, but the General Assembly has expressed concern at the serious threat to the territorial integrity and sovereignty of these territories constituted by the aggressive policies of the present régime in the Republic of South Africa.[1] The future of Gibraltar is clouded by the dispute between Spain and the United Kingdom.

In these last examples, the principle of self-determination and the right to independence clashes with the principle of territorial integrity.[2]

Patterns of history are particularly relevant. In past centuries, states, empires, federations, etc., grew up by conquest and expansion, by the use of force in fusing small (and not so small) territorial units into larger ones. After a certain time, and the use of peaceful, or not so peaceful, methods of assimilation, the small component units lost their international

[1] General Assembly resolution 2134 (XXI) of 29 September 1966.
[2] General Assembly resolution 1514 (XV) of 14 December 1960 on decolonization, *para 2*: All people have the right to self-determination; by virtue of that right they freely determine their political status and freely pursue their economic, social and cultural development; *para. 6*: any attempt aimed at the partial or total disruption of the national unity and the territorial integrity of a country is incompatible with the purposes and principles of the Charter of the United Nations.

identity forever. Nowadays, coercion is not used so freely, and conquest is not so easily condoned. As a result, the small territories which have managed to survive as independent states, as autonomous areas or even as dependent units, stand a better chance of remaining separate. Also, outside efforts at peaceful persuasion to organize larger and more viable groupings of emerging small territories have not been particularly successful in recent years.

Homogeneity of language, culture, civilization, standards of living, may also contribute to keeping a small territory intact. But many examples show that lack of homogeneity is not sufficient to undo a small territory: Guyana, Fiji, Mauritius, French Somaliland, etc.

No single factor can explain the drive of a small population to remain separate and its success in achieving that goal. It is generally a combination of factors: isolation, language, religion, social and cultural patterns, such economic elements as standards of living, state of development of agriculture and industry, foreign trade, monetary and fiscal policies. In addition, it is not merely the existence of any one factor or combination of factors, but the intensity and duration of these factors. And, as mentioned above, the existence or the creation of a feeling of homogeneity or common interest is another key element.

Outside reaction to the existence of a small territory is also to be taken into consideration: Liechtenstein, San Marino, Monaco, the Cook Islands, the Maldive Islands, Nauru, Western Samoa, Vatican City (Holy See), are accepted by the outside world as independent or internationally autonomous areas, for a variety of reasons. Many larger (and possibly more viable) parts of larger states, federations or confederations which might conceivably wish to secede, would in normal circumstances not now be considered by the outside world as entitled to any form of international recognition. So that even the question of which small territory had or has the right of self-determination is not always so simple to answer.

PART II: STATUS, PROBLEMS AND DIFFICULTIES OF SMALL STATES AND TERRITORIES

CHAPTER ONE

GENERAL

Many of the difficulties of most small states and territories are directly related to under-development in general: lack of resources, inadequate cadres, illiteracy, etc. These difficulties are not exclusive to small states and territories, but are very similar to those encountered in larger developing countries. In some cases, however, problems of under-development can affect mini-states in a different way than larger countries.

In addition, many handicaps of the small territories originate specifically in aspects of their "mini" condition: physical isolation, small area and population, etc. For instance, physical isolation and difficulty of communication will normally result in psychological isolation and a lack of knowledge or understanding of the outside world. A population may be so small that it becomes extremely difficult or exorbitantly expensive to establish institutions which would be indispensable in moulding a group into a viable nation. It may be impossible to organize a higher education system if there is not a minimum supply of students, or to set up a diplomatic service if enough people cannot be spared to fill the necessary posts.

The paucity of human or physical resources can reach a level beyond which the most elemental needs cannot be fulfilled at reasonable cost. A country of 10 million may have as few as one doctor for 100,000 inhabitants yet still have a minimal public health system if 100 doctors, including some specialists, can man one central and a few local health centres. But this setup would be impossible in a country of 100,000 inhabitants or less which had only one doctor.

Some of the difficulties of size are so obvious that there is hardly any need to dwell upon them. But one should not lose sight of the fact that some very small states, because of a favourable geographical location, or natural resources, or some other reason, have successfully consolidated their existence while at the same time continuously improving the lot of tneir people.

The solution to many problems of small territories is often closely linked with the political status of that territory or the evolution of that status. Some small territories have reached, somehow, a status equilibrium which has been preserved for a long period of time and has made it possible for them to function more or less satisfactorily. This is the case for old and stable European mini-states such as Luxembourg, Iceland, Liechtenstein, Monaco, San Marino and Andorra, or territories such as the Isle of Man and the Channel Islands. It is also more or less the case for territories such as Tonga, Bhutan and Sikkim. But in the great majority of cases, mini-states have reached their independence, or semi-independence, only recently, and are still searching for solutions to their problems in the context of their changed status. Or, in the case of small, non-independent territories, most of them are still under some form of colonial status from which they are trying to emerge, in the wake of the general trend towards decolonization which has characterized the middle of the twentieth century. And this raises for them a great number of questions.

A look at a list of small states and territories with populations of one million or less reveals that out of ninety-six countries listed, more than half are considered by the United Nations as Non-Self-Governing Territories, whereas only twenty-four are independent (of which seventeen are Members of the United Nations), the remainder being in an in-between, more complex, status.

Clear-cut distinctions in status are not always easy to make. But the watershed in political status may very well be determined by the answer to the following question: to what extent can the people themselves, alone, either unilaterally or as equals in negotiations, decide to change their status? The answer will be different for the independent states, some of the states in association and the protected states when compared with all the others (the majority of which are Non-Self-Governing Territories) for which a change of status has to be granted or agreed upon by an outside authority.

The evolution from dependent to independent status, and the various ways in which the population of a small territory can exercise its right to self-determination, will be briefly examined in a subsequent chapter. But it may be useful to underline at this stage that the problems of self-determination of small territories raise other delicate questions of a different nature: secession, fragmentation and territorial integrity.

The question has been posed why, if insignificant territories with minute populations should gain the right to self-determination and ultimately independence, large chunks of independent countries with sizeable populations should not be granted the same right, if this is truly the wish of the majority of the peoples of those areas? Philosophically, the question is a valid one. Politically, it is a doubtful one, at least from a United Nations point of view. Secession is the internal decision taken by part of a country against the country as a whole, a country which is internationally recognized as an indivisible entity. On the other hand, self-determination applies to the fate of an area which already holds to some degree a recognized separate international existence.

There may be cases where self-determination and secession appear to converge: e.g., from the point of view of Portugal, the independence of Guinea (Bissau), which it considers a province and an integral part of Portugal, would be secession. However, from the point of view of the United Nations, which has formally declared Guinea (Bissau) to be a Non-Self-Governing Territory within the meaning of Chapter XI of the Charter, independence, or whatever other departure from its status as a Portuguese province, would be the exercise of the unalienable right of self-determination.

From a United Nations point of view, it should not usually be very difficult to distinguish self-determination from secession, although there are cases where the distinction is less than completely clear. Is Anguilla, for instance, a secessionist territory in the unitary state in association with St. Kitts-Nevis-Anguilla, or is it a portion of a Non-Self-Governing Territory affirming its right to self-determination?

From a non-United Nations point of view, self-determination of small territories may sometimes smack of secession. This explains why some very outspoken anti-colonial countries sometimes have qualms about the independence of very small territories and their membership in the United Nations.

A more general problem is that of fragmentation. If self-determination is accepted at a given time, not only for existing dependent areas, but also for their component parts (for example, the ex-West Indies Federation and the various islands it included), is there any limit to the fragmentation which might result from the application of this principle? Already, tiny Anguilla (6,000 inhabitants) wants to leave St. Kitts-Nevis-Anguilla (61,000 inhabitants), which is a unitary state in association with the United Kingdom, and tinier Barbuda (1,200 inhabitants) may be contemplating the same vis-à-vis Antigua (60,000 inhabitants).

Excessive fragmentation is undesirable, of course, and should not be encouraged. To what extent can it be avoided when there are potent centripetal socio-political forces at work? The danger of fragmentation should not be overestimated: measures of decentralization and local autonomy often satisfy the small groups involved. Furthermore, one should distinguish between self-determination of small entities already in existence and self-determination of sub-units which do not yet have any recognized status. Unlike the latter, the former do not have to prove that they have the right to self-determination.

While the problem of fragmentation is usually raised with regard to the dangers of the future, the problem of territorial integrity refers to the past. To what extent is self-determination always compatible with territorial integrity? When a small territory was detached from a large one some centuries ago, and the original population displaced by newcomers, is self-government, or the wishes of the recently established population, to be the determinant element in deciding the future, or should the small territory be reunified with the country of which it constituted previously an integral part?

Both principles can be found in the same United Nations resolutions. For instance, General Assembly resolution 1514 (XV) states in paragraph 2 that "all peoples have a right to self-determination and by virtue of that right they freely determine their political status and freely pursue their economic, social and cultural development." But paragraph 6 of the same resolution affirms that "any attempt aimed at the partial or total disruption of the national unity and the territorial integrity of a country is incompatible with the purposes and principles of the Charter of the United Nations."

The question was debated many times in the United Nations in connexion with the status of Gibraltar (a narrow peninsula of 5.8 sq. km. on the southwest coast of Spain, with an estimated population of 25,000 inhabitants, under British administration since the Treaty of Utrecht of 1704). The United Kingdom stated that this was a problem of decolonization, and that the wishes and interests of the people of Gibraltar should be paramount. Spain felt that "continued British presence on a portion of Spanish soil was tantamount to the dismemberment of Spanish national unity and territorial integrity,"[1] and that furthermore the true population of Gibraltar had been expelled after 1704 and replaced by an extraneous population, composed of a wide variety of people whose descendants could not be considered the only legitimate indigenous inhabitants of the Rock.[2]

Similarly, Ifni, an African enclave administered by Spain, is claimed by Morocco on the basis of territorial integrity, rather than on the basis of self-determination.

The cases of British Honduras *vis-à-vis* Guatemala, the Falkland Islands *vis-à-vis* Argentina and Hong Kong and Macao *vis-à-vis* China raise similar problems.

[1] A/6700/Add.9, p. 15, para. 40.

[2] The problem of the rights of a newly immigrated community is looked upon differently in the case of Fiji, where the original population of Fijians, now a minority, is considered by the Administering Power (United Kingdom) as having a special entitlement to protection, whereas others are of the opinion that the entire population, including the majority Indian community, should be put on an equal footing of one man one vote, in spite of the fact that it established itself in Fiji only in fairly recent times.

CHAPTER TWO

STATUS AND INTERNATIONAL RELATIONS OF SMALL STATES AND TERRITORIES

A. PLACE OF THE SMALL TERRITORIES IN THE WORLD—EVOLUTION FROM COLONIAL STATUS TO INDEPENDENCE

Some people find it difficult not to display a certain amount of impatience with the nationalistic tendencies of micro-territories, those "unwanted and useless remnants of empires," at a time when larger, prosperous and long-established countries get together in common markets and aspire to gradual political unification. Socially and economically, it is probably advantageous to belong to a larger unit, and with present technological changes in communications, it is the inevitable trend. However, it is equally essential to understand that successful evolution in this direction is generally possible only if it is genuinely desired and understood by the peoples themselves, and if they are psychologically prepared for the change. Attempts to unite or federate little nations are doomed to failure if the efforts are imposed from the outside (even with the best of intentions), and if there has not been a long and thorough preparation of the populations. It has taken centuries for Europe to move very slowly and cautiously towards a certain degree of integration. The European countries concerned are far from being ready to lose their identity at a fast pace. It is therefore neither fair nor realistic to expect too much willingness on the part of the mini-territories, particularly those emerging into nationhood after a long period of dependence, to be rushed into co-operative arrangements which they are not ready to accept immediately as truly desirable.

The general symptoms of the growing "nationalism" of small, emergent countries indicate very clearly that no durable formulas of association will be arrived at without delays, trials and errors. In the meantime, one must be patient and accept seemingly unrealistic or absurd situations. Enlightened international public opinion should be wary of underestimating the intensity of feeling in small emergent territories.

In the past, a great number of states have been very small, yet viable and active. Needless to say, circumstances were quite different, and the multiplicity of small, independent political units during the Middle Ages or the Renaissance is not a very convincing argument for the perpetuation or creation of small states now.

Since then, with the industrial and social revolutions and the profound changes in communications, most of these small European political units have been integrated in larger political systems. A few have survived for one reason or another, but only by establishing special relationships with neighbouring "giants" have they been able to resist the centripetal forces of Europe since the nineteenth century: Luxembourg and its relations to Belgium and to the Netherlands, Monaco to France, Liechtenstein to Switzerland, San Marino to Italy.

The majority of small political entities, particularly in Europe, have simply been absorbed into greater entities and have disappeared from the international map. In Africa, the Pacific, the Caribbean and elsewhere, however, another solution prevailed for numerous areas, many of which had had only scanty relations with the Western world. They became colonial territories, and in that sense small islands and small continental areas took their place in international life, as subordinate entities. Although this turn of events deprived those territories of their freedom, they were brought into contact with the outside world and cultures other than their own.

Most very small territories were, until less than ten years ago, or are still now, parts of the colonial system. It is the liquidation of that system, started after World War II and extended now to these small entities, which has provoked some interest in their fate and a search for new solutions to the growing desire of their people to establish new relations with the rest of the world, without sacrificing their own personality.

In order to examine the status of small states and territories more specifically, a list has been made up of all areas which now have a more or less separate internationally recognized status, or which have had such status until very recently. This list is limited to territories with a population of one million or less.

The ninety-six territories listed present a wide variety in status from the point of view of international law. Seventeen are fully independent and are Members of the United Nations. Many others are Non-Self-Governing Territories for which the administering Powers accept a measure of international accountability under Chapter XI of the United Nations Charter (twenty-nine territories), or under the Trusteeship System (two territories). In other cases, the administering Power does not accept international accountability. Many territories which belong in neither the independent nor the colonial category have found permanent or temporary solutions in association, protection, federation or integration type arrangements, as well as other types of status which are difficult to classify. Insofar as possible, information on status is based on United Nations documents and data. Where a controversy exists, an attempt has been made to give the differing viewpoints.

The following Table does not purport to be an authoritative, juridical or exact classification of the small territories according to status. It may be argued that some of the territories mentioned should have been classified differently and that others should not have been included at all. The table is merely a rough guide to illustrate the complexity and the variations in the present situation.

TABLE VII—STATES AND TERRITORIES WITH A POPULATION OF ONE MILLION OR LESS: CLASSIFICATION ACCORDING TO STATUS

Name	Location	Land area sq. km.[a]	Population mid-1966 UN estimates[b]	Status	Recent UN action
AFRICA					
			I. Non-Self-Governing Territories		
1. Ifni	West Africa	1,500	53,000	Province of Spain, according to the administering Power. Claimed by Morocco. Spain has agreed to the principle of self-determination. Agreement in principle with Morocco has been announced on 10 Oct. 1967 on the practical implementation of GA resolution on Ifni.[c]	GA res. 2354 (XXII), 19 Dec. 1967, on decolonization of Ifni in consultation with Morocco. Annual examination by Committee of 24.
2. Spanish Sahara	West Africa	266,000	48,000	Spanish province, according to the administering Power. Claimed by Morocco and Mauritania. Spain has agreed to self-determination.	GA res. 2354 (XXI), 19 Dec. 1967, inviting Spain to hold a referendum under UN auspices, in consultation with Mauritania and Morocco. Annual examination by Committee of 24.

[a] Based on UN Statistical Yearbook 1966, Table 17.
[b] Based on UN Statistical Papers—Population and Vital Statistics, data available as of 1 July 1967.
[c] On 4 January 1969, Spain transferred Ifni to Morocco.

TABLE VII—(continued)

Name	Location	Land area sq. km.[a]	Population mid-1966 UN estimates[b]	Status	Recent UN action
AMERICA					
3. British Honduras (Belize)	On the Caribbean coast of Central America	22,965	109,000	British colony claimed by Guatemala. Mediation since 1965. Proposals made in 1968 by the mediator were unacceptable to British Honduras and UK Governments. Negotiations between Guatemala and UK in progress. UK ready to grant independence.	Statements in GA by UK and Guatemala on their respective positions. Latest confirmation that negotiations in progress: Guatemala in GA (A/PV.1680, p. 58-60, 3 October 1968). Annual examination by Committee of 24.
ASIA					
4. Brunei	NW part of Borneo	5,765	104,000	British protected state. Did not join the Federation of Malaysia in 1963.	Information annually before the Committee of 24.
EUROPE					
5. Gibraltar	Peninsula on SW coast of Spain	6	25,000	British colony claimed by Spain. UK organized referendum on 10 Sept. 1967. 12,138 voted in favour of retaining links with UK, 44 voted in favour of return to Spanish sovereignty.	GA res. 2353 (XXII), 19 Dec. 1967, declared that the holding of the referendum was a contravention of previous GA resolutions and invited the Governments of Spain and UK to resume negotiations. Annual examination by Committee of 24.

OCEANIA

6. Papua	SE part of New Guinea	222,998	601,000	Australian dependent territory administered jointly with the Trust Territory of New Guinea.	GA res. 2348 (XXII), 19 Dec. 1967, reaffirming previous resolutions requesting decolonization, elections on universal adult suffrage basis, fixing of early date for independence. Annual examination by Committee of 24.

ATLANTIC OCEAN

7. Bermuda	Islands in Western Atlantic Ocean	53	50,000	British colony.	GA res. 2357 (XXII), 19 Dec. 1967, on decolonization. Annual examination by Committee of 24.
8. Falkland Islands (Malvinas) and Dependencies	Islands in the South Atlantic Ocean	11,961	2,000	British colony. Claimed by Argentina. Negotiations between UK and Argentina under way.	Consensus approved by GA (XXII) on 19 Dec. 1967, inviting UK and Argentina to negotiate (A/7013). Annual examination by Committee of 24.
9. St. Helena and Dep. Ascencion Is. Tristan da Cunha	Islands in the South Atlantic Ocean	122 / 88 / 104 / 314	5,000 / 530 / 285 / 5,815	British colony.	GA res. 2357 (XXII), 19 Dec. 1967, on decolonization. Annual examination by Committee of 24.

TABLE VII—(continued)

Name	Location	Land area sq. km.[a]	Population mid-1966 UN estimates[b]	Status	Recent UN action
CARIBBEAN					
10. Bahamas	Islands in the Caribbean	11,406	140,000	British colony.	GA res. 2357 (XXII), 14 Dec. 1967, on decolonization. Annual examination by Committee of 24.
11. Cayman Is.	Island in the Caribbean	259	9,000	id.	id.
12. Montserrat	Island in the Caribbean	98	14,000	id.	id.
13. St. Vincent	id.	388	90,000	id. To become State in association with UK (Constitution of 22 Feb. 1967). Statehood day, scheduled for 29 May 1967, has been postponed.	id.
14. Turks and Caicos Is.	Islands in the Caribbean	430	6,000	British colony.	id.
15. British Virgin Is.	id.	153	9,000	id.	id.
16. U.S. Virgin Islands	id.	344	50,000	Unincorporated territory of the United States of America.	id.

INDIAN OCEAN

17. British Indian Ocean Territory	Four groups of islands in the Indian Ocean detached in 1965 from Mauritius (Chagos Archipelago) and from Seychelles (Aldabra, Farquhar, Desroches)	74	2,000	British colony.	GA res. 2232 (XXI), 20 Dec. 1966, on decolonization [para. 4 states that any attempt aimed at a partial disruption of national unity and territorial integrity of colonial territories and the establishment of military bases and establishments in these territories is incompatible with purposes of the Charter and GA res. 1514 (XV)]. Reiterated in GA res. 2357 (XXII), 19 Dec. 1967, para. 4. Annual examination by Committee of 24.
18. Cocos (Keeling) Islands	Islands in the Eastern Indian Ocean	14	1,000	Territory administered by Australia.	GA res. 2357 (XXII), 19 Dec. 1967, on decolonization. Annual examination by Committee of 24. id.
19. Seychelles	Islands in the Western Indian Ocean	404	49,000	British colony.	

PACIFIC OCEAN

20. American Samoa	Islands in the South Pacific Ocean	197	27,000	Unincorporated territory of the United States of America.	id.

TABLE VII—(continued)

Name	Location	Land area sq. km.[a]	Population mid-1966 UN estimates[b]	Status	Recent UN action
21. Fiji	Islands in the South Pacific Ocean	18,169	478,000	British colony.	GA res. 2350 (XII), 10 Dec. 1967, reaffirms need to send visiting mission to Fiji, and urges UK Govt. to reconsider its decision not to receive mission. Reaffirms previous resolutions calling for elections (one man, one vote) and the fixing of an early date for independence. Annual examination by Committee of 24.
22. Gilbert and and Ellice Islands	id.	886	54,000	id.	GA res. 2357 (XXII), 19 Dec. 1967, on decolonization. Annual examination by Committee of 24.
23. Guam	Island in the Western Pacific Ocean	549	77,000	Unincorporated territory of the United States of America.	id.
24. New Hebrides	Islands in the South Pacific Ocean	14,763	70,000	Dependent territory French/United Kingdom condominium.	id.
25. Niue Island	Island in the South Pacific Ocean	259	5,000	New Zealand dependent territory.	id.

Territory	Description			Status	Examination
26. Pitcairn Island	id.		5	British colony.	id.
27. British Solomon Islands	Islands in the South Pacific Ocean	29,785	140,000	British protectorate.	id.
28. Tokelau Islands	id.	10	2,000	New Zealand dependent territory.	id.

II. Trust Territories

Territory	Description			Status	Examination
29. Trust Territory of the Pacific Islands	Islands of Micronesia (Marianas Carolines and Marshalls) in the Pacific Ocean	1,779	94,000	Strategic Trust Territory under U.S. administration.	Annual examination by Committee of 24. Annual examination by Trusteeship Council; report of Trusteeship Council annually submitted to the Security Council.

III. Dependent Territories for Which No Information Has Ever Been Sent or Requested Under Chapter XI of the Charter
(Non-Self-Governing Territories)

Territory	Description			Status	
30. Christmas Island	Island in the Eastern Indian Ocean	135	3,000	Australian dependent territory (until 1957, it was part of the British Colony of Singapore. In 1958, it became a separate colony and was transferred to Australia).	—
31. Norfolk Island	Island in SW Pacific	36	1,000	Australian dependent territory.	—

TABLE VII—(continued)

IV. Non-Self-Governing Territories According to United Nations Decisions; But United Nations Jurisdiction Disputed by Administering Power

Name	Location	Land area sq. km.[a]	Population mid-1966 UN estimates[b]	Status	Recent UN action
32. Cabina (enclave of)	West Africa Atlantic coast, North of Congo River	7,270	60,000	Administrative district of Angola (with some manifestations of separatist movement). Angola is a Portuguese overseas province, according to the administering Power.	Considered by UN as a Non-Self-Governing Territory (as part of Angola)—GA res. 1542 (XV), 15 Dec. 1960. SC res. 218 (1965), 23 Nov. 1965. GA res. 2270 (XXII), 17 Nov. 1967, on self-determination for Portuguese territories.
33. Cape Verde Islands	Islands on the west coast of Africa	4,033	228,000	Overseas province of Portugal, according to the administering Power.	id.
34. Portuguese Guinea or Guinea-Bissao	West coast of Africa	36,125	529,000	id.	id.
35. Sao Tomé and Principe	Islands on the west coast of Africa	964	59,000	id.	id.
36. Macao	South coast of mainland China	16	250,000	id.	id.

37. Timor	Eastern part of island east of Indonesia	18,990	560,000	id.	id.
38. French Territory of the Afars and Issas (formerly French Somaliland)	East Africa	22,000	125,000	French overseas territory, not recognized by France as a Non-Self-Governing Territory since 1957. Referendum held on 19 March 1967; 22,555 voted in favour of continued association with France; 14,666 against.	Included in 1965, by the Committee of 24, in list of territories to which GA res. 1514 (XV) on decolonization applies. GA res. 2228 (XXI), 20 Dec. 1966, on decolonization: requested UN presence at referendum. France ignored UN resolution. GA res. 2356 (XXII), 19 Dec. 1967, regretted lack of co-operation of administering Power and urged independence at early date.
39. Namibia (Southwest Africa)	Southern Africa on South Atlantic coast	824,292	584,000	Formerly League of Nations Mandate under South African administration.	GA res. 2145 (XXI), 27 Oct. 1966, terminated mandate. GA res. 2248 (S-V), 19 May 1967, established UN Council for South-West Africa (now UN Council for Namibia). Independence to be attained by June 1968. Resolution not accepted by South Africa (A/6822). GA res. 2325 (XXII), 16 Dec. 1967, condemned refusal of South Africa to comply with GA resolutions.

TABLE VII—(continued)

Name	Location	Land area sq. km.[a]	Population mid-1966 UN estimates[b]	Status	Recent UN action
			V. States in Association		
40. Antigua	Island in the Caribbean	442	60,000	State in association with the UK since 27 Feb. 1967.	GA res. 2357 (XXII), 19 Dec. 1967, on decolonization. Annual examination by Committee of 24. On 6 October 1967, Committee of 24 took note of the constitutional developments in these territories, considered that they represented a certain degree of advancement in the political field, but reaffirmed that GA res. 1514 (XV) and other relevant resolutions continued to apply fully to these territories.
41. Dominica	id.	751	68,000	id. 1 March 1967.	id.
42. Grenada	id.	344	97,000	id. 3 March 1967.	id.
43. St. Kitts-Nevis-Anguilla	id.	357	61,000	id. 27 February 1967.	id.
Anguilla		100	6,000	[Anguilla seceded on 11 July 1967. Situation unresolved.]	

44. St. Lucia	id.	616	103,000	id. 1 March 1967.	id.
45. Cook Islands	Islands in the South Pacific	234	21,000	Self-governing territory with special association with New Zealand since 4 August 1965, after election held on 20 April 1965 under UN supervision.	GA res. 2064 (XX), 16 Dec. 1967, considered that the Cook Islands have attained full self-government, and reaffirmed the responsibility of UN to assist the people of the Cook Islands in the eventual achievement of full independence, if they so wish, at a future date.

VI. Protected States

46. Tonga	Island in the Pacific	699	75,000	British protected State.	
47. Bahrein	Island in the Persian Gulf	598	193,000	id.*	—
48. Qatar	On the Persian Gulf	22,014	71,000	id.*	—
49. Trucial States (or Trucial Oman)	South of Persian Gulf	83,600	130,000	Seven sheikhdoms with special relationship with UK.*	Relations with UK discussed by Committee of 24 in same context as Muscat and Oman (see A/6300/Add.8, Chapter 13, para. 7).

* Federation being formed in 1968.

TABLE VII—(continued)

Name	Location	Land area sq. km.[a]	Population mid-1966 UN estimates[b]	Status	Recent UN action
50. Muscat and Oman	Eastern corner of Arabia	212,379	565,000	Sultanate with special relationship with UK.	GA res. 2302 (XXII), 12 Dec. 1967, on decolonization, deploring the refusal of the UK to implement GA res. 1514 (XV) on decolonization and res. 2073 (XX) on the question of Oman (objecting to the colonial presence of the UK in that territory).
51. Bhutan	Eastern Himalayas	47,000	750,000	State in special treaty rerelationship with India (Treaty of 1949).	—
52. Sikkim	id.	7,107	180,000	State in special treaty relationship with India (Treaty of 1950).	—
VII. Parts of Recently Formed Federations					
53. Surinam	NE coast of South America	142,822	345,000	Autonomous and equal part of the Kingdom of the Netherlands (since	GA res. 945 (X), 15 Dec. 1955, approving cessation of transmission of infor-

		Area	Population	Status	Remarks
54. Netherlands Antilles	Two groups of islands in the Caribbean	961	210,000	1954). Member of UPU and WMO.	mation under Article 73 e of the Charter.
55. Sabah	North coast of Borneo	76,115	551,000	id. Member of UPU and WMO. State within the Federation of Malaysia (since 16 September 1963). Claimed by the Philippines.	id. Fact-finding mission of the Secretary-General in August-September 1963 (see A/5801, pp. 26–28).
56. Sarawak	NW coast of Borneo	125,205	862,000	id.	id.
57. West Cameroons	West Africa	43,000	826,000 (1958)	Southern part of the Trust Territory of the Cameroons under British administration; joined Republic of Cameroun to form Federal Republic of Cameroon (1 October 1961) after UN-supervised plebiscite on 11 February 1961.	GA res. 1608 (XV), 21 April 1961, terminating Trusteeship Agreement.

VIII. Territories with Special Sovereignty Arrangements

		Area	Population	Status	Remarks
58. Ryukyu Islands	Group of islands in the NW Pacific	2,196	944,000	Under U.S. military administration but residual sovereignty with Japan (Art. III, Japanese Peace Treaty of 1952).	—

TABLE VII—(continued)

Name	Location	Land area sq. km.[a]	Popula-tion mid-1966 UN esti-mates[b]	Status	Recent UN action
59. Panama Canal Zone	Central America	1,432	56,000	Territory leased to U.S. since 1903 with full sovereignty rights. Negotiations now under way between Panama and U.S. Panama claims sovereignty.	Listed in 1946 as Non-Self-Governing Territory by the U.S. As a result of protest by Panama on 14 November 1946, U.S. ceased transmitting information under Article 73 e of the Charter.
IX. Partly Integrated Territories with Special Status					
60. Isle of Man	Island in the Irish Sea	588	50,000	Territory belonging to the Crown. Part of the British Isles, but not of the United Kingdom.	—
61. Channel Islands (Jersey and Guernsey)	Islands off the NW coast of France	195	115,000	Remaining parts of Duchy of Normandy, belonging to the Crown. Part of the British Isles, but not of the United Kingdom.	—
X. Provisionally Integrated Territories					
62. West Irian	Western part of New Guinea	412,781	800,000	Under Indonesian administration since 1 May	GA res. 1752 (XVI), 21 Sept.1962, noting the agree-

| | | | | ment between the Netherlands and Indonesia. | 1963, on basis of agreement between the Netherlands and Indonesia of 21 Sept. 1962. Freedom of choice to be exercised with UN participation before the end of 1969. |

XI. Overseas Territories Integrated with Metropolitan State

				Status	Transmission of information under Chapter XI discontinued since 1947.
63. Guadeloupe and Dependencies	Islands in the Caribbean	1,779	319,000	Classified by France as overseas department (1946), integral part of French Republic.	
64. Martinique	id.	1,102	327,000	id.	id.
65. French Guiana	NE coast of South America	91,000	37,000	id.	id.
66. Réunion	Island in W. Indian Ocean	2,510	408,000	id.	id.
67. St. Pierre-et-Miquelon	Islands in N Atlantic off south coast of Newfoundland	242	5,000	French overseas territory (1946), integral part of French Republic.	id.
68. New Caledonia and Dependencies	Islands in SW Pacific	19,000	93,000	id.	id.

TABLE VII—(continued)

Name	Location	Land area sq. km.[a]	Population mid-1966 UN estimates[b]	Status	Recent UN action
69. French Polynesia	Islands in S. Pacific	4,000	90,000	French overseas territory (1946), integral part of French Republic.	Transmission of information under Chapter XI discontinued since 1947.
70. Comoro Archipelago	Islands in SW Indian Ocean	2,171	225,000	id.	Transmission of information under Chapter XI discontinued since 1957. The working group of the Ctte. of 24 proposed in 1967 and in 1968 that this territory be included in the list of territories to which GA res. 1514 (XV) on decolonization is applicable. (A/AC.109/L.392 and L.525.) The Ctte. of 24 deferred a decision on this question (A/AC.109/SR.510, 19 April 1967 and A/AC.109/SR.647, 4 November 1968).
71. Wallis and Futuna Is.	Islands in S. Pacific	200	8,000	id.	—
72. Faroe Is.	Group of islands in N. Atlantic	1,399	37,000	Self-governing community within Kingdom of Denmark.	—

XII. States Members of the United Nations

73. Luxembourg	Western Europe	2,586	335,000	1815	24 Oct. 1945	—
74. Iceland	Island in N. Atlantic	103,000	195,000	1 Dec. 1918	19 Nov. 1946	—
75. Congo (Brazzaville)	West Central Africa	342,000	850,000	15 Aug. 1960	20 Sept. 1960	—
76. Cyprus	Island in Eastern Mediterranean	9,251	603,000	16 Aug. 1960	20 Sept. 1960	SC res. 186 (1964), 4 March 1964, on peace-keeping, and 254 (1968), 18 June 1968.
77. Gabon	West Central Africa	267,667	468,000	17 Aug. 1960	20 Sept. 1960	—
78. Trinidad and Tobago	Islands off N. coast of South America	5,128	1,000,000	31 Aug. 1962	18 Sept. 1962	—
79. Kuwait	On the Persian Gulf	16,000	491,000	19 June 1961	14 May 1963	—
80. Malta	Islands in the Mediterranean	316	317,000	31 May 1964	1 Dec. 1964	—
81. The Gambia	West coast of Africa	11,295	336,000	18 Feb. 1965	21 Sept. 1965	—

TABLE VII—(continued)

Name	Location	Land area sq. km.ᵃ	Population mid-1966 UN estimatesᵇ	Independence	UN Member since	Recent UN action
82. Maldive Islands	Islands in the Indian Ocean	298	101,000	26 July 1965	21 Sept. 1965	—
83. Guyana	NE coast of South America	214,969	662,000	26 May 1966	20 Sept. 1966	—
84. Botswana	Southern Africa	569,581	580,000	30 Sept. 1966	17 Oct. 1966	GA res. 2063 (XX), 16 Dec. 1965. Fund for Economic Development of Bechuanaland, Basutoland and Swaziland. GA res. 2134 (XXI), 29 Sept. 1966, expressing concern about aggressive policies of South Africa.
85. Lesotho	id.	30,344	865,000	4 Oct. 1966	17 Oct. 1966	
86. Barbados	Island in the Caribbean	430	245,000	30 Nov. 1966	9 Dec. 1966	—
87. Mauritius	Islands In Western Indian Ocean	2,096	780,000	12 Mar. 1968	24 Apr. 1968	—
88. Swaziland	Southern Africa	17,363	390,000	6 Sept. 1968	24 Sept. 1968	GA res. 2063 (XX) and 2134 (XXI), see above.
89. Equatorial Guinea	West Africa on the Gulf of Guinea	28,051	272,000	12 Oct. 1968	12 Nov. 1968	Elections in August-September 1968 under UN supervision.
Rio Muni		26,017	198,000			
Fernando Poo		2,034	74,000			

XIII. States Not Members of the United Nations, But Members of Specialized Agencies

	Area			Status	Specialized Agencies	
90. Holy See (Vatican City State)	Area of Rome	0.44	1,000	Sovereign State recognized by treaties and Concordat with Italy (1929).	IAEA, UPU, ITU. Observer's office at UN Hdqtrs.	—
91. Liechtenstein	Europe	157	19,000	Independent Principality (1806)	UPU, ITU, ICJ.	—
92. Monaco	id.	1.5	23,000	id. (1861)	IAEA, UNESCO, WHO, UPU, ITU, Observer's office at UN Hdqtrs.	—
93. San Marino	id.	61	18,000	Independent Republic (1862)	UPU, ICJ	—
94. Western Samoa	Islands in the South Pacific	2,842	130,000	Independent State since 1 Jan. 1962 after UN supervised plebscite on 9 May 1961.	WHO, ECAFE	GA res. 1626 (XVI), 18 Oct. 1961, terminating Trusteeship Agreement and expressing hope that Western Samoa would be admitted to membership in the UN should it so desire.

TABLE VII—(Continued)

XIV. States Not Members of United Nations or Specialized Agencies

Name	Location	Land area sq. km.[a]	Population mid-1966 UN estimates[b]	Status	Recent UN action
95. Andorra	Europe	453	11,000	Co-Principality (President of French Republic and Bishop of Urgel, Spain).	—
96. Nauru	Island in the Pacific Ocean	21	6,000 (of which 3,100 are Nauruans)	Independent since 31 January 1968.	GA res. 2347 (XXII), 19 Dec. 1967, terminating Trusteeship Agreement upon accession of Nauru to independence on 31 January 1968.

Category I lists twenty-eight Non-Self-Governing Territories, with an indication of their present status and the most recent United Nations involvement or action. In many cases, changes in status are under consideration.

Category II contains the only mini-Trust Territory.

Category III lists two territories which are not technically Non-Self-Governing Territories, but could nevertheless be included under this heading.

Category IV lists eight territories which, from the United Nations point of view, are Non-Self-Governing, but where the administering Power disagrees and does not accept any jurisdiction by the United Nations.

Category V lists six territories where recent association arrangements have come into being which, according to the administering Power, remove them from the category of Non-Self-Governing Territories. For five of them, the United Nations has not been actively involved in this change of status and considers that General Assembly resolution 1514 (XV) on decolonization still applies.

Category VI lists seven cases where the relations with a distant or neighbouring country are of the protective type, but are outside the Non-Self-Governing sphere of Chapter XI of the Charter. Situations in this category vary widely.

Category VII lists five cases of small territories involved in recently formed federations (with either distant or neighbouring territories). It might be argued that in these cases no element of separate international status remains, and that they should not have been listed. They are included here because some of them are individual members of specialized agencies, because the federative arrangements of others have not been readily accepted by neighbouring countries or because there was a special United Nations involvement from which something can be learned.

Category VIII lists two special situations of sovereignty arrangements.

Category IX again refers to two other special situations which are hard to classify.

Category X is a case which, from the United Nations point of view, is unique.

Category XI lists ten territories, nine of which are French overseas territories and departments, which are integrated with the metropolitan Power.

Category XII lists the seventeen Members of the United Nations with a population of one million or less.

TABLE VIII—(Continued)

III. Small Territories Which have Lost Since 1945 Whatever International Status They May have had (and are no longer relevant to the study)

Name	Location	Land area sq. km.	Popula-tion	Former status	Present status	Recent UN action
6. Saar	Europe	2,559	984,000 (1947)	International territory, 1919–1935, 1945–1956	Integral part of German Federal Republic since 1 January 1967.	—
7. Trieste	id.	773	365,000	Envisaged as free territory by 1947 peace treaty with Italy.	Since 1954, one zone is under Italian civilian administration, the other under Yugoslav civilian administration.	
8. Greenland	Island in the North Atlantic	2,175,000 (of which 342,000 free of ice)	41,000	Non-Self-Governing Territory until 1952.	Integral part of Denmark since 1953.	GA res. 849 (IX), 22 Nov. 1954, noting the achievement of self-government by integration with Denmark.
9. Tangier	NW tip of Africa	350	183,000 (1955)	International zone (1923–1956).	Integral part of Morocco since 1956.	—
10. British Somaliland	East Africa	176,120	650,000 (1958)	British Protectorate until 1960.	Joined with Trust Territory of Somaliland under Italian adminis-	—

11. British Togoland	West Africa	34,000	423,000 (1954)	Trust Territory under British administration until 1957.	tration to form independent Republic of Somalia on 1 July 1960. Joined with Gold Coast to form independent State of Ghana on 6 March 1957, after UN-supervised plebiscite on 9 May 1956.	GA res. 1044 (XI), 13 Dec. 1956, terminating Trusteeship Agreement.
12. Northern British Cameroons	id.	17,500	774,000 (1958)	Northern part of Trust Territory under British adm. until 1961.	Joined Federation of Nigeria as part of Northern Region on 1 June 1961, after UN-supervised plebiscites on 9 Nov. 1959 and 11–12 Feb. 1961.	GA res. 1608 (XV), 21 April 1961, terminating Trusteeship Agreement.
13. Zanzibar	Two islands off East coast of Africa	1,658	340,000 (1958)	Independent State from 9 Dec. 1963 to 26 April 1964.	Part of United Republic of Tanzania (after merger with Tanganyika on 26 April 1964).	Separate Member of the UN from 16 Dec. 1963 to 26 Apr. 1964.
14. Alaska	NW part of North American continent	1,518,000	226,000 (1960)	Non-Self-Governing Territory. Unincorporated Territory of the U.S. until 1959.	State of the United States of America since 3 January 1959.	GA res. 1469 (XIV), 12 Dec. 1959, stating that Alaska and Hawaii had exercised the right of self-determination.
15. Hawaii	Islands in N. Pacific	16,600	632,000 (1960)	id.	id. since 21 Aug. 1959.	

TABLE VIII—(Continued)

Name	Location	Land area sq. km.	Population	Former status	Present status	Recent UN action
16. Goa (also Damoa and Diu)	Enclaves in India	4,200	650,000 (1959)	Portuguese Province until 1961. Considered by UN as Non-Self-Governing Territory (GA res. 1542 (XV), 15 Dec. 1960, not accepted by Portugal).	Union Territory of India since December 1961.	No action taken by Security Council on Portuguese complaint in 1961.
17. Sao Joao Batista de Ajuda	West Africa	0.02	1	Portuguese enclave in Dahomey, administered from Sao Tomé and Principe. Covered by GA res. 1542 (XV), as indicated above.	United with Dahomey in 1961.	—
18. French Establishments in India (Chandernagor, Pondicherry, Karikal, Mahé, Yanaon)	Enclaves in India	500	323,000 (1952)	French overseas territory.	Transferred to India in 1950 and 1954 as Union Territory.	—

ment of a degree of self-government generally follows a comparable pattern.

In British-administered territories, features of self-government normally appear in the form of legislative and executive organs, which are first consultative, and whose competence and composition grows by leaps and bounds. The members of the legislative organs are at first appointed. Later, some of them are elected; then a majority and finally all are elected, at first under a restrictive electoral system and ultimately under a system of universal suffrage, with or without special arrangements for certain segments of the population.

The legislative body becomes increasingly competent, but the Governor or chief representative of the colonial authority keeps powers of disallowance. Finally, only selected fields such as defence and foreign affairs are withheld from the legislative assembly. A similar evolution takes place for the executive organs; at an early stage, there is direct administration by expatriate officials, aided by advisory bodies. Ultimately, there is a ministerial system. At some point, after contact with representatives of the indigenous population, after constitutional conferences and elections or a referendum, independence is granted, or special association relationships are agreed upon. The organs of the new country are usually patterned on those of the former metropolitan country, Britain. In the remnants of the British Empire, the pace of this evolution, as well as the logistics, varies from territory to territory.

In French-administered territories, a similar evolution has taken place; however, the pattern of institutions is more uniform, and centralized, and changes affect most territories simultaneously. A specific feature is inclusion of the territory in the French Union and later in the French Community, and finally, either full independence or integration in the French Republic as an overseas department or territory.

Portuguese territories have moved from colonial status to an integrated status as overseas provinces in a centralized system. But Spanish territories, which were first destined to be overseas provinces, now seem to move towards self-determination and possibly independence.

Some territories have moved from partial self-government to full partnership in an existing or new federal system (Dutch territories).

In other cases, pre-existent forms of self-government have been maintained within protection arrangements.

The evolution of small territories has usually been slower than larger colonial territories because of less pressure within the territory, less sense of urgency in the metropolitan country and a lower priority in the concern of the international organizations. Recognition of the special needs and problems of smallness has come relatively late, and a search for new solutions has been undertaken only recently in the metropolitan countries as well as in the international organizations. Solutions such as federative arrangements have generally failed. However, full independence in very small states often has features which are different from those in large states.

It is not necessary in this study to examine in detail the various aspects of the development of self-government in small states and territories as far as internal institutions are concerned. What matters is the international status of these territories and their special relations, if any, with the administering Power, former administering Power, protector country, federation or union to which they belong. Also of concern is conduct of foreign affairs, maintenance of security and participation in international and regional organizations.

Separate chapters are devoted to these questions.

As has been indicated, many formulas for self-government or independence have been tested in small countries. The status of these countries is changing steadily. Theoretically, each situation constitutes an option for the individual small state or territory. In fact, however, many of these options are physically, legally or economically impossible or undesirable. Therefore, the actual options in a given case may be few. On the other hand, options which have never been tried out may be worth considering.

Different forms of autonomy or self-determination may in fact be very similar. Examples: in the unitary state of Tanzania, Zanzibar may have as much autonomy as has West Cameroon in the Federal Republic of Cameroun; relations between the independent state of Nauru and Australia may be similar to those between the self-governing territory of the Cook Islands and New Zealand.

Independence is a crucial point in the evolution. However: (a) it is a relative concept, subject to many variations; (b) one aspect of independence is the fact of free choice. If the people have a choice of options, including the possibility of "going it alone," they have enjoyed a moment of independence, regardless of their final choice. Real self-determination is therefore at least synonymous with temporary independence. This aspect is more important from a United Nations point of view than the classical notion of independence, because it marks the watershed in United Nations responsibilities *vis-à-vis* dependent territories; (c) formal independence may be only a temporary choice, future options remaining open. But post-independence choices are generally considered outside the scope of United Nations responsibility.

A few examples will illustrate the diversity of status among small states and territories.

A distinction has to be made between dependent small territories where the administering Power has accepted the obligations of Chapter XI of the Charter and of General Assembly resolution 1514 (XV), and those where the administering Power does not recognize the United Nations view that these provisions should apply. In the first category, the evolution is uneven. In some instances, the administering Power is instrumental in moving the people towards self-government. In others, it claims that the population is not ready for a change, is perfectly happy with its status and resents being prodded from the outside. In both cases, however, a dialogue with the United Nations exists. In the second category, that dialogue does not exist.

*   *   *   *

An example of a Non-Self-Governing Territory recognized as such by the administering Power, but until recently rather far from self-government, is a group of thirty-seven islands spread over 5 million sq. km. in the Pacific: the *Gilbert and Ellice Islands.* The estimated total population in mid-1966 was 54,000. These islands came under the jurisdiction of the High Commissioner for the Western Pacific in 1877 and were declared a British Protectorate in 1892. By an Order of 10 November 1915, they were annexed and became the Gilbert and Ellice Islands Colony.

Responsibility for the administration of the territory rests with the High Commissioner for the Western Pacific, who resides outside the territory in the Solomon Islands. This responsibility is deputized to a Resident Commissioner, who is the chief administrative officer of the territory and who lives in the capital of the territory (Tarawa). The High Commissioner and the Resident Commissioner are both empowered to make laws for the peace, order and good government of the territory, with due regard to local custom. In cases where a proposed law might affect the lives of the population, the Island Council is consulted.[1] An Executive Council was established in 1963, presided over by the Resident Commissioner and consisting of the Assistant Resident Commissioner and not more than seven other members (three official and four unofficial) appointed by the Resident Commissioner, subject to the power of revocation vested in the High Commissioner. The Executive Council had advisory powers only. An Advisory Council, consisting of the Resident Commissioner and eleven unofficial appointed members, was created at the same time, to be consulted at the discretion of the Resident Commissioner or the High Commissioner.

Thus the legislative and executive powers are entirely in the hands of the colonial Power, although local councils in the various islands can make some local regulations. This less advanced system of government prevailed some decades ago in most colonial territories, but is no longer to be found in more advanced territories. The low degree of political advancement in the Gilbert and Ellice Islands has been attributed to the remoteness of the islands, poor communications with the outside world and among the many small islands, lack of homogeneity of the popula-

[1] A/6700/Add. 13, p. 6. See also Sir Kenneth Roberts-Wray, "Colonial and Commonwealth Laws," pp. 902-903.

tion,[2] lack of political awareness of the islanders and their lack of interest in playing a more active rôle. In August 1967, however, a new Constitution was approved. It provided for a Governing Council to replace the Executive Council, with five official and five elected members holding legislative powers, and a House of Representatives consisting of not more than thirty members, twenty-three of them elected on the basis of universal adult suffrage, responsible for advising the Governing Council on proposed legislation. The new Constitution is particularly interesting because it exemplifies a new pattern of constitutional development in some of the smaller British territories—an experiment in which executive and legislative powers are being conferred upon a single body (the Governing Council).

The economic resources of these low-lying coral atolls are meagre. The only commercial crop is copra. Ocean Island, the only volcanic island, has rich deposits of phosphate rocks, which, at the present rate of exploitation, will be exhausted within thirteen years. The phosphate industry is controlled by the Phosphate Commissioners (Australia, New Zealand and the United Kingdom), as was until recently the case for Nauru, 160 miles to the west.

In 1945, the owners of Ocean Island, about 2,000 Banabans, left their island, and have since lived 1,200 miles away on Rabi Island (in the Fiji group), which was bought for them out of their share of the phosphate royalties. These royalties go to both the Banabans (as landowners) and the Gilbert and Ellice Islands Colony. They constitute the major revenue of the colony. Under an agreement reached in 1960, the colony received 23sh. a ton on Ocean Island phosphate, and the Banabans received 2sh. 8d. (1965 production: 360,000 tons). In 1966, these royalties were raised to 35sh. 1d. and 7sh. respectively. In addition, the United Kingdom promised to make an *ex gratia*, once for all, payment of £80,000 to the Banabans in consideration of the effects of mining upon Ocean Island since 1960.

The Banabans, who do not consider themselves part of Fiji, refused to participate in elections held in Fiji in 1966. In 1968, they expressed their desire to secede from the Gilbert and Ellice Islands and attain independence for their island (which they have inhabited for less than twenty years). They nave petitioned the United Nations to that effect.[3] This development gave rise to strong protest by the elected members of the Gilbert and Ellice Islands, who stated that they themselves "were on the certain path to independence, and did not wish to be thwarted in that

    [2] The Ellice people are reputed to be somewhat suspicious of the Gilbertese. They consider themselves closer to the Fijians and Samoans, whereas the Gilbertese may feel closer to the Marshallese of the Trust Territory of the Pacific Islands.
    [3] A/AC.109/PET.967.

purpose by being deprived, through fragmentation or dismemberment of their territory, of economic resources of any one part at the request of absentee owners whose sole purpose was to secure for themselves undue wealth to the detriment of the rest of the territory."[4]

The outlook for the Gilbert and Ellice Islands is generally considered gloomy, particularly after the phosphate of Ocean Island is exhausted. Tourism appears to hold some promise for the future. A team of experts, appointed by the Ministry of Overseas Development in the United Kingdom, conducted a socio-economic survey of the islands at the end of 1967.

* * * *

In *Fiji* self-government is more advanced than in the Gilbert and Ellice Islands. This colony has a different problem. Although it comprises over 800 islands and islets in the Pacific Ocean, 90 per cent of the total land mass is contained in two large islands, where the great majority of the population lives. That population was estimated in mid-1966 at 478,000, of which 41 per cent is Fijian, 50 per cent Indian (descendants of indentured Indian labourers imported at the end of the 19th century to work on the sugar plantations), and the remainder European, part European, Chinese or members of other Pacific races.

Fiji's Constitution was promulgated on 23 September 1966 and is based on the agreement reached at a Constitutional Conference held in 1965.

Executive power is vested in the Governor, who is appointed by the Queen. Defence, external affairs, internal security and the Public Service are reserved to the Governor at his discretion and as his special responsibility. The Executive Council of ten members has four official members and six elected members, appointed by the Governor from among the elected members of the Legislative Council. In September 1967, the Executive Council became a Council of Ministers with executive powers. The Governor is required to consult the Executive Council, except on the subjects specifically reserved to him. On other matters he is required to accept its advice, except when he considers it necessary to act against such advice in the interest of public order, public faith or good government. In such cases, he is required to seek approval of the Secretary of State.

The Legislative Council consists of thirty-six elected members and four official members nominated by the Governor. Elections are based on universal adult suffrage in a system designed to ensure representation to the various communities: fourteen Fijians, twelve Indians, and ten who are neither Fijian nor Indian. The majority in each such group (twenty-seven) is elected on a communal roll restricted to electors of that group; a minority (9) is elected by a cross-voting system, each member being

[4] A/AC.109/PET.986.

elected by voters of all communities in each of the three constituencies. The Legislative Council has power to make laws on any matter, subject to certain restrictions. The Governor is empowered to refuse assent or to reserve legislation.

This complicated electoral system is intended by the administering Power to reassure the Fijian and Indian communities that neither group shall dominate. The problem is to "find a framework in which people of different races, proud of their distinct cultural heritages and ways of life, could live together in peace, friendship and co-operation." The situation is complex and delicate, and the administering Power takes the view that the premature introduction of a single electoral roll throughout the territory, as recommended by the United Nations,[5] would do more harm than good.

The leader of the Opposition stated in the Legislative Council that the Constitution had been imposed upon the Indian community against the will of its representatives, and that it was undemocratic, iniquitous and unjust.

The administering Power considers that Fiji's problems stem not from a lack of resources, nor from remoteness or smallness of population or geographical area, but from the presence of several communities which are racially, culturally and even economically diverse. A complicating factor is that the two largest communities are equal in numbers. Another complication is that one of the communities consists of people who are deeply conscious of being indigenous to the territory. The administering Power did not agree to a visit to the territory by a United Nations mission, as had been recommended by the General Assembly.[6]

With its sugar and copra resources, an increasing number of tourists, a rich forestry potential, a five-year development plan, good communications with the outside world and a political consciousness, this fairly large island colony in the Pacific is considered fit for independence, yet it is wary of the possibilities of racial strife. A hopeful sign is seen in the establishment of multiracial political parties. At the United Nations, some believe that too much importance is being attributed to the racial composition of the population. Up to now, however, neither the administering Power nor the local government of Fiji has shown much enthusiasm for the United Nations recommendation of universal suffrage on a common roll, a visiting mission and the setting of an early date for independence.

*   *   *   *

The Gilbert and Ellice Islands are scattered over a large area and are only on the threshold of self-government. The population of Fiji is

---

[5] General Assembly resolution 2185 (XXI) of 12 December 1966.
[6] *Ibid.* Reaffirmed in General Assembly resolution 2350 (XXII) of 19 December 1967.

grouped more compactly on two large islands and enjoys a relatively advanced degree of self-government. *British Honduras* (or Belize) is part of the American continent, bounded by Mexico and Guatemala, on the Caribbean coast. Its area is 22,965 sq. km., and the estimated population in mid-1966, 109,000. Under its 1964 Constitution, the Governor, appointed by the Queen, is required to act in accordance with the advice of ministers in all matters except defence, external affairs, internal security and the public service. The Governor also has special responsibility in the sphere of finance for as long as the government of British Honduras continues to receive budgetary aid from the United Kingdom. The Cabinet consists of a Premier and other ministers who are members of the legislature and are appointed by the Governor on the advice of the Premier.

The legislature (National Assembly) is bicameral, consisting of a Senate and a House of Representatives. The Senate consists of eight members appointed by the Governor. The House of Representatives includes eighteen members elected by universal adult suffrage.

Forestry and agriculture are the mainstays of the economy.

The Government of Guatemala maintains that sovereignty over British Honduras (Belize) belongs exclusively to Guatemala and that the territory is an integral part of Guatemala. The United Kingdom states repeatedly that it has no doubts as to its sovereignty over the territory. In 1965, an American mediator was assigned to this long-standing dispute. His report, made public on 29 April 1968, proposed that the United Kingdom grant independence to British Honduras under the name of Belize not later than 31 December 1970. It also called for closer cooperation between Belize and Guatemala in foreign affairs, defence, communications and economic development. These proposals were not accepted by British Honduras, and consequently the United Kingdom stated that they were not acceptable to the British Government either.

Negotiations are continuing between the governments of Guatemala and the United Kingdom.

It seems that the situation can be summarized as follows: the United Kingdom is ready to grant independence to British Honduras; a majority of the inhabitants of British Honduras, fearing Guatemalan domination, want to stay British; Guatemala maintains its claim to the territory, a claim based particularly on Guatemala's need for access to a deep sea port in the Caribbean, without which its northern province will remain undeveloped.

* * * *

These three examples of Non-Self-Governing Territories (Gilbert and Ellice Islands, Fiji and British Honduras) illustrate the diversity of situations of small dependent territories. There is one more type: a dependent territory declared Non-Self-Governing by the United Nations but not recognized as such by the administering Power. As is well known,

Portugal considers all its overseas territories to be Portuguese provinces and refuses to accept their applicability to Chapter XI of the Charter, despite formal General Assembly resolutions on the subject.[7] With the exception of Angola and Mozambique, all the *Portuguese territories* have populations under one million: four in Africa—Cabinda (60,000),[8] Cape Verde Islands (228,000), Portuguese Guinea (also called Guinea-Bissao—(529,000)[9], Sao Tomé and Principe Islands (59,000), and two territories in Asia—Macao (250,000) and Timor (560,000). The Portuguese "provinces" in India (Goa, Damao and Diu—650,000 inhabitants) were retaken by India in 1961.

According to the Portuguese Constitution and the Overseas Defense Act of 1963, each overseas territory is a province of Portugal, subject to the authority of the central government but having its own territorial organs with limited powers and functions. Powers of legislation are entrusted to the organs of the central administration of the Portuguese Government in Portugal: the Portuguese Council of Ministers, the Corporative Chamber and the Overseas Council, the latter two being advisory bodies in which the overseas provinces are represented. There are other central advisory organs: the Conference of Overseas Governors and the Overseas Economic Conference. The territorial government is composed of a Governor, a legislative council with limited powers and a territorial advisory council. The legislative council is partially elected by a restricted electorate. For example, the legislative council in Portuguese Guinea, established in 1963, includes fourteen members, of whom three are *ex officio*, eight are elected by "organic groups" and three are elected directly. A similar situation prevails in Sao Tomé and Principe.

In Portuguese Guinea (as well as in Angola and Mozambique), the Native Statute was in effect until 1961. This Statute distinguished between "civilized" and "natives." The integration of the "natives" into the Portuguese pattern of local government and administration depended on their attaining the "state of development" deemed necessary for government by Portuguese civil law. Since 1961, Africans may theoretically opt to be governed by Portuguese civil law without having to meet any educational or cultural requirements. However, the basic philosophy remains: although the "natives" are a numerical majority, the small number of "originarios" from Portugal are considered to form the

---

[7] General Assembly resolution 1542 (XV) of 15 December 1960 and subsequent resolutions by the General Assembly and the Security Council.

[8] Cabinda is part of Angola, although it is physically separated from Angola by a strip of the Democratic Republic of the Congo. There have been secessionist moves made in Cabinda, and it is not inconceivable that Cabinda will go its own way. Rich reserves of exploitable oil have been found in this territory.

[9] Since 1963 there has been fighting in the territory, and part of this area is no longer under *de facto* Portuguese control.

"sociological majority," because they are considered to possess "enlightenment" and education. Therefore, they control political power, technological and economic development.[10] In smaller territories other than Guinea (Cape Verde, Sao Tomé and Principe, Macao and Timor), there is no such "cultural competition"; in the first two because the population is predominantly "mestiço," in Macao because it is "Luso-Chinese" and in Timor because it is "Luso-Indonesian-Malayan." Theoretically, the inhabitants of these territories have the same legal rights and obligations as citizens living in metropolitan Portugal.

* * * *

Are the mini-territories in the former *British West Indies* still Non-Self-Governing Territories, or are they mini-states in association, fully self-governing? The question was debated in the Committee of Twenty-Four and the General Assembly. The Committee "took note of the constitutional developments that have taken place in these territories, and considered that they represent a certain degree of advancement in the political field for the people concerned . . ." but reaffirmed that "resolution 1514 (XV) and other relevant resolutions continued to apply fully to these territories";[11] in other words, that the territories have not been fully decolonized.

To understand the situation in these islands, it is necessary to go back to 1958, when a Federation of British dependent states in the Caribbean was established by the United Kingdom. The idea of federating the British West Indies goes back to the beginning of the 20th century, when a number of inter-island institutions were set up: in 1919 a West Indian Court of Appeal, in 1924 an Imperial College of Tropical Agriculture and in 1934 a West Indian Trade Commission to Canada. Regional co-operation was encouraged by participation in the Caribbean Commission, established in 1942. After World War II, a number of conferences on federation were held, and in 1958 the United Kingdom established the Federation of the West Indies, comprising two large islands (Jamaica and Trinidad and Tobago) and eight small islands, the Leeward Islands (Antigua, St. Kitts-Nevis-Anguilla, Montserrat), the Windward Islands (Dominica, St. Lucia, St. Vincent, Grenada) and Barbados.

The Federation was conceived as a preliminary move towards independence; however, it failed. The larger islands withdrew, and the idea of federation collapsed altogether. Analyzing the causes of this failure, political scientists[12] observe that it was a federation created from outside: Britain played a major rôle, but the West Indians were not ready

[10] A/6700/Add.3. para. 64.

[11] A/6700/Add.14 (Part II), para. 1033, p. 133.

[12] Amitai Etzioni, *Political Unification*, Ch. V "A union that failed," New York, 1965.

to accept the idea of federation and West Indian nationhood. In addition, the fact that the federative constitution reserved many powers to the United Kingdom did not make the federation more popular. It was planned to let the federation become fully independent only after some years. In the meantime, the United Kingdom gradually increased the self-governing rights of the islands at a rate which varied from island to island, the larger islands receiving it at an earlier date. Another difficulty which confronted the federation was the fact that over half of the population of the federation lived in Jamaica, and almost 80 per cent in Jamaica and Trinidad and Tobago. These larger islands were more autonomous and more economically developed, yet the federal constitution favoured the small islands.

As summarized by R. L. Watts,[13] "the chief characteristic of the federation was the niggardly list of legislative and executive powers assigned to the central government. These were restricted primarily to external relations, inter-island communications, the University and the West Indies Regiment. The central government's lack of financial resources and its dependence on a mandatory levy upon the territories dramatized its weakness: with one tenth the revenue of either Jamaica or Trinidad, it was hardly in a position to achieve the hoped for economic transformation. The West Indies Federation was also unusual among modern federations in commencing without a customs union or a common currency. Throughout its brief history the frail federation was undermined both by the weakness of the forces for integration and by the inadequacies of the federal structure itself. The absence of a sense of common identity except among a few of the educated middle classes, the relative looseness of inter-island organizations and associations, the extremely limited trade between the islands, the growing rather than diminishing differences in economic structure and level of development, and especially the lack of any feeling of urgency inducing collective action in the face of a common danger, prevented the growth of an integrating sense of community. Furthermore, the form of the federal structure itself contributed to its downfall. The scope of central authority was so restricted, its function so limited and its budget so minute that to most of the West Indians the Federation appeared to involve additional expenditure to no effective purpose. It was not surprising therefore that the major charismatic leaders in Jamaica and Trinidad, Manley and Williams, chose to remain as premier in their own islands, thus further emphasizing the relative insignificance of federal politics. The support of the two largest islands, and particularly of Jamaica, was further alienated by their marked under-representation, not only in the federal parliament, but also as a result of the governing General Labour Party's failure in the two big islands at the 1958 federal elections in the Central Executive. An

---

[13] R. L. Watts, *New Federations—Experiments in the Commonwealth.*

important factor weakening the prestige of the central government was the rapid constitutional progress within the islands themselves, which left the central government by comparison, with a less advanced constitution. This gave the Federation the appearance of a brake rather than an aid to full political independence."

In 1961, Jamaica and Trinidad and Tobago decided to secede and became separate sovereign nations the following year. On 31 May 1962, the Federation was formally dissolved.

The remaining eight islands were then guided towards an East Caribbean Federation. However, Grenada soon withdrew from the negotiations and expressed more interest in uniting with Trinidad and Tobago.

In 1965, Antigua decided not to join the proposed federation of the seven remaining islands, and soon thereafter Barbados declared itself in favour of separate independence (which it eventually got on 30 November 1966). This ended the hopes for federation.

Following new rounds of talks with the islands, a new series of proposals for constitutional advance was made at the end of 1965 for the four Windward Islands (Dominica, St. Lucia, St. Vincent and Grenada) and two of the Leeward Islands (Antigua and St. Kitts-Nevis-Anguilla). The new formula offered each territory the opportunity to become a state in association with Britain, with the right to amend its own constitution and the right, should it so desire, to end the association and declare itself independent without further recourse to the British Parliament. The association could also be terminated by Britain. External affairs and defence would continue to be the responsibility of the British Government. Entrenched clauses in the new constitutions would safeguard democratic institutions and procedures. A regional Supreme Court would adjudicate for the region. Problems of future regional co-operation would be discussed later. Britain considered that this new concept of complete internal self-government, together with the right to become fully independent at will, represented the termination of the old colonial relationship.

Agreement on these lines was reached at separate conferences. The association between Britain and each state is described as free and voluntary. The agreement provides that as a guarantee of its voluntary nature it is terminable at any time by either party (Britain has undertaken to give six months' notice of intention to terminate). On termination of association, the state will become fully independent of Britain, but while the association continues, neither side will be able to amend its terms without the agreement of the other. As a safeguard against hasty or ill-considered legislative action, an interval of ninety days must elapse between introduction of legislation in an associate state to terminate and any consideration of it; such legislation requires the approval of two thirds of the persons voting in a referendum before the legislation is submitted for assent. However, in order not to hinder the formation of a new federation, no referendum is required if the proposal is to terminate association with Britain in favour of association with some other Commonwealth country in the Caribbean. It was further decided that if need arose, the states would continue to be eligible for budgetary aid.

The new statute was approved in the United Kingdom on 16 February 1967, and came into effect on 27 February 1967 for Antigua and St. Kitts-Nevis-Anguilla; on 1 March for Dominica and St. Lucia; on 3 March for Grenada. It was scheduled to come into effect on 29 May for St. Vincent, but the date was postponed because of an electoral dispute and a change of government due to new elections.

The United Kingdom representative in the Committee of Twenty-Four described associated statehood "not strictly speaking as an alternative to independence but rather a status of self-government which includes the open option of independence."

A majority of delegations in the Commitee of Twenty-Four expressed reservations about the new status. Most were based on the procedure according to which the colonies had become associated states. To what extent had the views of the people been accurately ascertained? No referendum had been held. No general elections had taken place to the organs, with the members of which consultations had been held. No other alternatives had been put before the population. The United Nations had not been associated with this change, and the United Nations request to visit the territories had been turned down. Some felt that the requirement of a two-thirds majority for a subsequent choice of independence was a limitation to freedom of choice. For these and other reasons, the Committee reaffirmed that General Assembly resolution 1514 (XV) continued to apply fully to these territories; in other words, that they had not yet been properly decolonized. The United Kingdom, on the other hand, continued to maintain that these territories were now fully self-governing, could become unilaterally independent and were therefore no longer under the jurisdiction of the Committee of Twenty-Four.

In spite of the collapse of attempts to create a viable federation, however, the wish to organize some activities on a regional basis is still very much alive in the territories of the former British West Indies. Plans have been made for a regional development bank. Regional development projects, in such fields as fisheries, meteorology and education, have been started. A Caribbean Free Trade Association (CARIFTA) has been recently established, and there has been talk of a Common Market. The West Indies Associated States have been accepted as a single associate member of ECLA. The University of the West Indies has campuses in Jamaica, Trinidad and Barbados, and there is even a combined West Indies cricket team.

*   *   *   *

During the debates on the Eastern Caribbean Islands, comparisons were repeatedly made with the situation in the *Cook Islands,* the "decolonization" of which was endorsed by the General Assembly. This small territory, comprising two groups of islands scattered over 2 million sq. km. in the South Pacific, and with a population of some 21,000 inhabitants, was first a British protectorate, then a colonial part of New Zealand. In 1963, the representative bodies of the Cook Islands, who were searching for a change of status, rejected "the alternatives of complete independence, integration with New Zealand, and a Polynesian federation" and demanded a régime of full self-government, continued association with New Zealand and retention of New Zealand citizenship. New Zealand kept the United Nations informed of these projects, which had culminated in a new draft constitution. In keeping with the spirit of General Assembly resolution 1514 (XV), New Zealand invited the United Nations to supervise the general legislative elections to be held early in 1965 (since the chief issue would be the future of the territory), as well as to observe debates on the constitution by the newly elected Legislative Assembly. The United Nations appointed a representative who, with an appropriate United Nations staff, supervised the electoral campaign and the elections held on 20 April 1965. The United Nations representative also witnessed the constitutional development that followed, *inter alia,* the adoption of the new constitution in May 1965.

Upon the report of the United Nations Commissioner to the General Assembly, the General Assembly adopted resolution 2064 (XX) on 16 December 1965, which declared that the Cook Islands had attained full internal self-government and were no longer a Non-Self-Governing Territory. It rejected a proposal to delete the reference to the fact that "from 4 August 1965 the Cook Islanders have had control of their internal affairs and of their future."

But it included in the resolution a clause reaffirming "the responsibility of the United Nations, under General Assembly resolution 1514 (XV) to assist the people of the Cook Islands in the eventual achievement of full independence, if they so wish, at a future date."[14] The new status of the Cook Islands is in most respects the same as the one described above for the West Indian Associated States. The big difference is that in the first case, the United Nations was associated with the procedures of change of status, whereas in the other case, the United Nations was presented with a *fait accompli.* The Cook Islands Constitution provides for full self-government, but also continued association with New Zealand, under a common head—the Queen, and a common nationality—New Zealand. The conduct of the external relations of the Cook Islands remains the responsibility of the New Zealand Government. In some cases, New Zealand is expected to delegate to the Cook Islands Government the power to act on its behalf, and in others it should consult or inform the latter about its actions. Amendments to the constitution require a two-thirds majority; the people of the Cook Islands are thus

[14] General Assembly resolution 2064 (XX), 16 December 1965.

empowered to change unilaterally their status and opt for full independence.

*   *   *   *

Protected states have maintained their traditional régime and their system of internal self-government, but have placed themselves under the protection of a foreign power, which has usually taken over their foreign relations. The protected state retains its head of state, a king, sultan or sheikh, who does not relinquish his sovereignty. The Kingdom of *Tonga*, for example, has been under British protection since the end of the 19th century. In 1879, 1900, 1958 and 1968, treaties of friendship were concluded with the United Kingdom, but the centralized system of the Kingdom and the strong cultural and political cohesion of the Tongans made it possible to evade foreign colonization. British protection was accepted, as was supervision of foreign relations, but Tongan authority over domestic affairs was kept intact, and the number of foreigners in the Kingdom was strictly limited. The Government of Tonga has the right to make agreements of purely local concern, except in matters of defence, security and civil aviation, with neighbouring Pacific islands and with Australia and New Zealand, including arrangements for the exchange of representatives. It can also become a member of any international organization for which it is eligible. The Tongan Government has full control over its own finances. The late Queen Salote was a colorful and respected Head of State. She attended the coronation of Queen Elizabeth II in 1953, and the Duke and Duchess of Kent attended the coronation of King Tupou IV in 1967.

Tonga recently joined with Fiji, Western Samoa and the Cook Islands to form the Pacific Islands Producers Secretariat. Its aim is to co-ordinate primary production and marketing, but members have also begun to discuss wider questions, such as the possibility of a Common Market of Free Trade Association among themselves.

*   *   *   *

Among the states listed in the category of protected states, only Muscat and Oman (population estimates 565,000) and the Trucial States (population estimate 130,000), both on the southeast coast of the Arabic Peninsula, have generated interest and controversy in the United Nations.

Muscat and Oman are not technically speaking a British Protectorate, but are considered by the United Kingdom and other countries as an independent and sovereign state. However, British association with Muscat dates back to 1798, when a treaty was signed between Muscat and the East India Company. Present relations with the United Kingdom are governed by the Treaty of Friendship, Commerce and Navigation of 1951 and the exchange of letters of 1958. The United Kingdom enjoys extra-territorial jurisdiction over British subjects and protected persons. The British political agent (later Consul General) has over-all responsibility for the postal services and the telegraphic communications (Oman has no stamps of its own and uses over-printed United Kingdom stamps). The administration of airfields falls within the jurisdiction of the British Agent. British officers serve as cadre for the Omani forces, and the United Kingdom pays a subsidy towards development of roads, medical aid, educational facilities and an agricultural programme. There is a dispute concerning the relative powers of the Imam (now living in exile in Saudi Arabia) and the Sultan. The Imam, with his Higher and Revolutionary Councils, claims to direct the struggle of the people to regain independence, whereas the Sultan maintains that all the people of Oman are his subjects.

The situation in Oman was the subject of a visit by a representative of the Secretary-General in 1963. An *ad hoc* Committee of the General Assembly investigated the situation in 1964. In 1965, following debate, the General Assembly considered that "the colonial presence of the United Kingdom in its various forms prevented the people of the territory from exercising their rights to self-determination and independence,"[15] and called upon the United Kingdom to take measures to "eliminate British domination in any form." The United Kingdom took the position that the Sultanate of Muscat and Oman was an independent and sovereign state, that Article 2 (7) of the Charter prohibited the United Nations from intervening in the domestic affairs of any state and that there were no military bases in the Sultanate, except two Air Force staging posts.

The General Assembly reaffirmed its stand in 1966[16] and 1967.[17]

* * * *

There are three federative arrangements in which mini-territories have become part of larger federations. In each case, the United Nations has been involved and has given its blessing to the new arrangements:

Surinam and the Netherlands Antilles in the Kingdom of the Netherlands;

Sabah and Sarawak in the Federation of Malaysia;

West Cameroon (southern part of the former Trust Territory of the Cameroons under British administration) in the Federal Republic of Cameroun.

Surinam, covering 142,822 sq. km. on the northeast coast of South America, had a mid-1966 estimated population of 345,000. The *Netherlands Antilles* (islands of Curaçao, Aruba and Bonaire, north of Venezuela, and islands of St. Eustatius and Saba and part of St. Maarten, east

[15] General Assembly resolution 2073 (XX), 17 December 1965.

[16] Based on UN Statistical Papers—Population and Vital Statistics, data available as of 1 July 1964.

[17] General Assembly resolutions 2238 (XXI), 20 December 1966, and 2302 (XXII), 12 December 1967.

of Puerto Rico) comprise a total land area of 961 sq. km. and have an estimated population of 210,000. In 1951, the Government of the Netherlands informed the United Nations that, following a promise of self-government made in 1942, and ensuing negotiations with the Legislative Council of the Netnerlands Antilles and Surinam, the Constitution of the Netherlands had been revised to permit the establishment of new relationships within the Kingdom. Each territory would henceforth manage its own affairs and look after their common interest jointly on an equal footing. Universal suffrage was introduced. Interim Orders of Government were enacted, giving these territories control over their internal affairs. In 1954, agreement was reached on a new charter for the Kingdom of the Netherlands. The Charter of 29 December 1954 states that the Kingdom of the Netherlands comprises three countries, each of which exercises autonomy in internal affairs. Decisions in Kingdom affairs are taken jointly on an equal basis; the three countries accord each other aid and assistance. Except in such matters as defence, foreign affairs and nationality, which are the prerogatives of the Kingdom, the three countries have exclusive authority to make final decisions. Moreover, each country can draw up and amend its own constitution. The Queen is the head of the Kingdom and of the three countries, and the Kingdom and the countries all have a parliamentary system of government. Statutes for the Kingdom are enacted by the Netherlands Parliament, which acts for this special function as Parliament of the Kingdom. However, the Parliaments of Surinam and the Netherlands Antilles can influence the decisions of the Netherlands Parliament. The executive power in external affairs is vested in the Council of Ministers of the Kingdom, in which the Antilles is represented by a Minister plenipotentiary who has full voting powers.

On 15 December 1955, the General Assembly adopted resolution 945 (X), in which it took note of the fact that "the peoples of the Netherlands Antilles and Surinam had expressed, through their freely elected representative bodies, their approval of the new constitutional order" and that "cessation of transmission of information under Article 73 e of the Charter was appropriate"; in other words, that these territories were no longer Non-Self-Governing.

*   *   *   *

Sabah (population 530,000) and Sarawak (population 838,000) are two parts of the island of Borneo. In 1961, a proposal to create a Federation of Malaysia was made by the Prime Minister of the Federation of Malaya. The new Federation would include the Federation of Malaya, the Crown colonies of Singapore, Sarawak and Sabah (North Borneo). This idea originated in a reluctance to federate with Singapore, which, it was felt, might have upset the delicate racial (Malayan, Chinese) balance in Malaya. After the Cobbold Commission made an investigation of this matter, it was decided that Singapore, Sarawak and Sabah would obtain independence by joining the Federation of Malaysia on 31 August 1963. The Governments of the Philippines and Indonesia, having their own claims on Sarawak and Sabah, stated that they would welcome the formation of Malaysia provided that the support of the people of these territories was ascertained. Agreement was reached between the Governments of Indonesia, the Philippines and the Federation of Malaya to request the Secretary-General to ascertain, prior to the establishment of the Federation of Malaysia, the wishes of the peoples of Sabah and Sarawak. The purpose was to ensure complete compliance with the principles of self-determination, as embodied in General Assembly resolution 1541 (XX), and to ascertain whether the elections which had recently taken place in the two territories had been free and properly held and whether the formation of the new Federation of Malaysia had been the major issue in these elections. The date of the federation was postponed to 16 September 1963. The Secretary-General communicated his favourable findings on 14 September.

The protected State of Brunei decided to remain outside of the Federation. Singapore seceded from the Federation on 21 September 1965.

*   *   *   *

The case of the *Trust Territory of the Cameroons* under British administration is quite *sui generis*. This former mandated territory had been administered in two separate parts. The southern part, following the introduction of federal government in Nigeria in 1954, was constituted as a self-governing region of the Federation of Nigeria, with its own executive council and legislature. The northern part remained administratively part of Nigeria's Northern Region, with no personality of its own. In view of the approaching independence of Nigeria, plebiscites were held in both areas under United Nations supervision to ascertain whether the population wished to join Nigeria or the Republic of Cameroun. In 1961, the northern part of the Trust Territory elected to join with the Federation of Nigeria. As a result, this area became an indistinguishable part of Nigeria, merging with the various administrative portions of the Northern Region of Nigeria.

The southern part, however, elected to join the independent Republic of Cameroun as a constitutive part of the new Federal Republic. As West Cameroun, it kept its individuality. This was the first instance when a federation was formed out of a formerly French-administered part and a formerly British-administered part. Many complications have ensued, but the Federal Republic of Cameroun is slowly and progressively overcoming them.

The termination of the Trusteeship Agreement on the two parts of the Cameroons under British administration was approved by the General Assembly in resolution 1608 (XV) of 21 April 1961.

*   *   *   *

The French Overseas Departments and Territories constitute a special category of mini-territories.

The *French Overseas Departments* are Martinique (1,090 sq. km., population, 321,000), Guadeloupe and island dependencies (1,700 sq. km., population, 316,000), French Guyana (88,000 sq. km., population, 36,000) and Réunion (2,510 sq. km., population, 397,000). All four have been French possessions since the middle of the 17th century, except for short periods of time. They were considered as colonies, and in 1946, French listed them as Non-Self-Governing Territories, about which it intended to transmit information under Article 73 e of the Charter. It was pointed out, however, that this information was transmitted without prejudice to the future status of the territories concerned.

Subsequently, in 1947, France discontinued sending information on these territories, explaining that under the French Constitution of 27 October 1946, establishing the French Union, the Overseas Departments, which for more than a century had participated in French political life and had asked for complete assimilation, had been granted a régime which was largely identical with that of the departments of metropolitan France. The whole of metropolitan legislation had been extended to these new departments, and it was no more possible to speak of dependence than it would be in the case of a province in relation to the State of which it formed part.

It was similarly contended that some of the *Overseas Territories,* that is, New Caledonia and dependencies (18,700 sq. km., population, 91,000), the French Establishments in Oceania, later called French Polynesia (4,000 sq. km., population, 80,000) and St. Pierre-et-Miquelon (242 sq. km., population, 5,000) had also been provided with régimes which on the whole closely resembled those of the Overseas Departments of metropolitan France as regards the status of the inhabitants and their method of political representation, and that they also could no longer be regarded as Non-Self-Governing Territories.

Under the 1946 Constitution, metropolitan France and the Overseas Departments and Overseas Territories were all part of the French Republic, which together with the Associated Territories (the territories under the International Trusteeship System) and the Associated States (Laos, Cambodia, Viet-Nam, Morocco, Tunisia) formed the French Union. In addition to participating in the central organs of the Union and the French Republic, each Overseas Territory had an elected assembly of its own. All nationals of the Overseas Territories had the status of citizens in the same capacity as French nationals; however, special laws determined the conditions under which they could exercise their rights as citizens.

The United Nations took no action on France's ceasing to transmit information on its Overseas Departments and on some of its Overseas Territories.

France continued to transmit information under Article 73 e of the Charter on some other Overseas Territories which were not yet fully self-governing, including French West Africa, French Equatorial Africa, Madagascar, tne Comoro Archipelago (2,170 sq. km., population, 220,-000), French Somaliland (23,000 sq. km., population, 81,000)[18] and the New Hebrides (14,750 sq. km., population, 68,000).

Under a new Constitution of 4 October 1958, the French Union was replaced by a Community. The Overseas Territories could either retain their status under the 1946 Constitution as an integral part of the Republic, or they could become Overseas Departments of the Republic or member states of the Community. The new Constitution was approved by referendum on 28 September 1958 by metropolitan France and by all Overseas Departments and Territories (except Guinea). After that, most of the Overseas Territories (Madagascar, Sudan, Senegal, Mauritania, Chad, Gabon, Middle Congo, Ubangi-Shari, Dahomey, Ivory Coast, Upper Volta, Niger) elected to become member states of the Community (and subsequently, in 1960, independent states and Members of the United Nations). Other Overseas Territories, namely, the three on which France had ceased to transmit information in 1947 (New Caledonia, French Polynesia, St. Pierre-et-Miquelon), as well as two which were no longer considered Non-Self-Governing Territories (French Somaliland and the Comoro Archipelago), chose to retain their previous status of Overseas Territories of the Republic. France then ceased transmitting information on the latter two territories, which it no longer considered Non-Self-Governing.

The United Nations took no action on the discontinuation of transmission of information until 1966. At that time, and particularly after the disturbances in French Somaliland in August 1966 and France's decision to hold a plebiscite in that territory, the United Nations, through its Committee of Twenty-Four on decolonization, again took an interest in the territory.

Under the present French constitutional arrangements, the French Overseas Departments (Martinique, Guadeloupe, Réunion and French Guyana) and the French Overseas Territories (New Caledonia, French Polynesia, Wallis and Futuna, St. Pierre-et-Miquelon, the Comoro Archipelago and French Somaliland) remain mini-territories which are an integral part of the French Republic and have no separate international status. In Martinique, Guadeloupe and Reunion, there are autonomist movements, the strength of which is subject to conflicting assessments.

The small Overseas Territory where the situation proved to be acute

[18] Recently given as 125,000, of which 37,000 are non-French citizens.

was French Somaliland (*Côte française des Somalis*). During the visit of General de Gaulle to Djibouti on 25 and 26 August 1966, demonstrations in favour of independence took place. Further disturbances took place in September. France then announced that a referendum would be held to decide the political future of French Somaliland. The United Nations General Assembly recommended that appropriate arrangements be made for a United Nations presence before and supervision during the referendum (General Assembly resolution 2228 (XXI) of 20 December 1966). France did not accept that recommendation. On 19 March 1967, a referendum was held on the question "Do you wish the territory to remain part of the French Republic under a new local government?" 22,555 voted "yes," 14,666 "no."

The vote is said to have been largely on ethnic lines, Afars favouring ties with France, Somalis favouring unification with the Republic of Somalia. Some violence was reported, and the Somalis complained that a large number of Somalis were deprived of their right to vote and expelled from the territory.

The name of the territory was changed to "French Territory of the Afars and Issas." The new status includes a larger degree of autonomy for the territory.

On 19 December 1967, the General Assembly reaffirmed its views and urged France to co-operate fully with the Committee of Twenty-Four ". . . in accelerating the process of decolonization of the Territory and to grant independence to the inhabitants at an early date."[19]

*   *   *   *

The *Isle of Man* is an island situated in the Irish Sea. It is roughly equidistant from England, Ireland, Scotland and Wales. It was ceded by the King of Norway to the King of Scotland in the 13th century and later came under the English Crown.

The Isle of Man is not a part of the United Kingdom, nor is it a foreign dominion of the Crown. It is a dependency with a considerable degree of self-government. It is administered by the British Home Office, and is part of the British Isles. Manxmen are not represented in the British Parliament.

The Government of the island is headed by a Lieutenant-Governor who is appointed by the Crown and titled the Lord of Man. He is the supreme authority and commands the military forces and the police. There is a council, or Upper House, and a House of Keys, the Lower House. The two sit separately but come together to form a *Tynwald* or Court for certain matters. It should be noted that the House of Keys forms one of the most ancient legislative assemblies in the world. The island's legislature is competent to make laws on all subjects, including its own constitution. It is subject to United Kingdom Acts; however, they do

[19] General Assembly resolution 2356 (XXII), 19 December 1967.

not apply to the island except by express provision or necessary implication. In practice, the United Kingdom Parliament does not legislate for the island in local matters unless there is some special reason to do so, e.g., when it is convenient for the British Isles to be subject to a uniform statute. In such circumstances, the practice nowadays is for the Act to be extendable by Order-in-Council, with exceptions, modifications and adaptations.

Manx finances are separate from those of the United Kingdom. The main revenues are from customs duties. Power to determine the customs duties is conferred on the *Tynwald* and is subject to an agreement to keep in line with the United Kingdom. The *Tynwald* controls the revenue spending and appoints Boards (education, agriculture, fisheries and local government) to administer the affairs of the island. There are no death duties, and income taxes are less than those imposed on other British subjects. In 1961, the Isle of Man issued its own bank notes for the first time. In 1968, the Union Jack was no longer flown from public buildings on official occasions, but was replaced by the Manx flag.

A working party was set up in 1967 to examine constitutional relationships between Britain and the Isle of Man. In July 1968, members of the *Tynwald* made it plain that they were impatient at the slow progress of the constitutional talks, and there was a move to appeal to the United Nations about United Kingdom interference in the island's affairs. No appeal was made, however.

The economy is largely dependent upon Britain, particularly through tourist trade. Every year, at least a half-million persons from all parts of the British Isles visit the island.

*   *   *   *

An example of self-government with a measure of integration is the *Faroe Islands*. This group of small islands in the North Atlantic Ocean forms a self-governing community within the Kingdom of Denmark.

These people are descendants of 9th century Norse settlers. A Norwegian king took possession of the islands in the 9th century, and in the 14th century they were taken over by Denmark. An active movement for self-government developed after 1910. In 1940, when the Germans invaded Denmark, the British took control of the islands until September 1945. Following this, Denmark proposed to seek the views of the islanders in a plebiscite. When the plebiscite was inconclusive (5,490 votes for independence to 5,656 against), the negotiations for independence were held in abeyance for two years. In 1947, these negotiations were renewed in Copenhagan, and, as a result, the islands obtained self-government, their own flag and a currency called the *krona*.

The Faroese constitute a separate nationality and have preserved numerous ancient customs and manners. Faroese, akin to Icelandic rather than Danish, is the main teaching language.

The self-governing unit has its own election rules, municipal institutions, sanitation, schools, social services, trade laws and taxation procedures. These and other matters are controlled by an executive (the *Landsstyre*) and legislature (the *Lagting*) which has twenty-seven members.

The Danish Government is represented by a Commissioner (the *Rigsombudsmand*) and, in turn, the Faroese elect two representatives to the Danish Parliament.

*   *   *   *

Among the small independent states, some have entered into special arrangements with other states.

Luxembourg entered into an economic union agreement with Belgium in 1922. The agreement, which is for fifty years, provides for the elimination of the customs barrier between the two countries and the use of both Belgian and Luxembourg currency in the Grand Duchy. In 1948, a customs union was established between the Belgium-Luxembourg economic union and the Netherlands, and the existing customs tariffs were superseded by the joint Benelux Customs Union Tariff. Luxembourg is a member of NATO, EEC, OECD and plays an active role in these regional inter-governmental organizations. It is also a founding member of the United Nations and participates in the activities of all the specialised agencies.

When Belgium, the Netherlands or Luxembourg is a member of the Economic and Social Council, the Member State includes in its delegation special counsellors from the two other States.

Luxembourg has deliberately not established a university, in order that students can widen their experience by going beyond the boundaries of the Granch Duchy.

*   *   *   *

The problems of *Cyprus* are due not to its size, but to the ethnic composition of its population (80 per cent Greeks, 18 per cent Turks) and to the historically strained relations between the two groups. Cyprus became independent in 1960, at which time the Constitution provided that the young Republic was to be headed by a Greek Cypriot president and a Turkish Cypriot vice-president. A Council of ministers (seven Greek and three Turkish) would assist in the exercise of the executive power. A Legislative House of Representatives, elected by universal suffrage, was to be 70 per cent Greek Cypriot and 30 per cent Turkish Cypriot. Separate communal chambers were also created. It was stipulated that Cyprus should not be united either wholly or in part with another state (which precluded *enosis* with Greece), and that it should not be subject to partition. The territorial integrity and the Constitution of Cyprus were to be guaranteed by Great Britain, Greece and Turkey. Greece and Turkey were allowed to maintain limited military contingents in Cyprus, while the Cyprus remained within the Sterling area and became a member of the Commonwealth.

In 1963, President Makarios proposed modifications of these constitutional arrangements, and violent clashes broke out between Greek and Turkish Cypriots. A United Nations peace-keeping force has been on the island since then.

*   *   *   *

The main problem of *Malta* is the dismantling of the British naval base and the reconversion of its economy. Malta, which became independent in 1964, is a member of the Commonwealth. Agreement on defence authorises British forces to remain in Malta for ten years, and financial arrangements provide for British capital aid for the development of Malta's economy. One of the measures taken is to convert the drydocks from naval to commercial use. There are plans for the establishment of a free port.

*   *   *   *

The Gambia is a small territory in West Africa lying on both sides of the Gambia River and surrounded by Senegal, except for about thirty miles of coastline. Consultations were held in 1962 between the Government of Senegal and the Government of The Gambia (with the consent of the Government of the United Kingdom) about "the possibility that on attainment of full sovereign independence by The Gambia some form of association might be entered into between The Gambia and Senegal." The Government of The Gambia also stated "that independence must provide an effective means of leading the Gambian people towards greater prosperity and well-being, and that for economic reasons The Gambia might find it difficult to sustain this objective as an isolated sovereign state; secondly, that independence when attained should contribute to the wider cause of African unity. In the light of these two principles and in view of the close economic, geographic and ethnologic links which bind the two countries, the Government decided that steps should be taken, after preliminary discussion with the Senegalese Government, to acquire the necessary information which would enable the Government and the peoples of The Gambia to consider the question of some form of association with Senegal on the attainment of independence. . . . At the same time, the Gambian and Senegalese Governments have recognized that due to the different traditions and culture on which Senegal and The Gambia have developed, and to the differing political, economic and fiscal systems which obtain in the two countries, the problems involved in achieving political and economic association are considerable."

In addition, the Premier of The Gambia emphasized "that in the event of any form of union between the two countries being agreed, the Gambia Government would wish to see reserved in any such agreement certain essential safeguards concerning the measure of autonomy which would be enjoyed by The Gambia after association. These matters would concern those which the Government would wish to retain under its own control in any association with Senegal and would include responsibility for internal administration, the police, civil service and local government; preservation of Gambian civil and criminal law, educational and professional standards and qualifications; and the maintenance of the close ties of association between The Gambia, the United Kingdom and the Commonwealth. They would also concern those matters which The Gambia would wish to consider sharing with Senegal (defence, foreign policy—including joint representation overseas—financial matters and development). Ancillary to these matters, the Gambia Government would also wish to see secure conditions ensuring joint representation for matters for which responsibility might be apportioned, conditions which would ensure continuance of The Gambia's trading remaining liberalized, and provision for some form of constitutional appeal to protect safeguards and conditions secured in any final agreement."

At the request of the Governments, the United Nations sent a team of four experts to look into the matter. Their report was released in 1964.

The experts advocated a process of association in successive stages, and considered that it might be more practical initially to limit the association to a treaty relationship establishing a common defence, common international representation and common organs to align trade, customs and development policies, and to facilitate mutual relations between the citizens of the two countries.

In 1965, The Gambia became independent and a member of the Commonwealth. The United Kingdom stated that there were no plans for a merger with Senegal, and that the question of closer association with Senegal was a matter for The Gambia to decide on its own. The Gambia and Senegal signed a number of agreements of co-operation (defence, foreign policy and development of the Gambia River), pending such time when a closer association would be instituted between the two countries. So far, the closer association remains somewhat theoretical, although a further treaty of association was signed in 1967 to "promote and expand the co-ordination and co-operation between The Gambia and Senegal in all areas." An inter-ministerial committee of the two states was also established; this committee meets occasionally to discuss matters of common interest. A Sene-Gambian federation still seems to be a distant dream.

The Gambia is a Member of the United Nations; it has no permanent Mission to the Organization. It sends *ad hoc* delegations to the General Assembly, and between General Assembly sessions it uses the Permanent Mission of Senegal as an intermediary for its relations with the United Nations.

*   *   *   *

The *Maldive Islands,* a former British protectorate in the Indian Ocean, have been independent since 1965. This Sultanate, which became a republic in November 1968, is the least populated Member of the United Nations, with only 101,000 people.

An agreement with the United Kingdom gives the United Kingdom unrestricted and exclusive use of one of the islands (Gan, in Addu atoll) and part of another island in the same atoll until 1986. It also has full rights to maintain armed forces there and to reactivate the war-time staging post.

In 1966, the United Nations Development Programme, at the request of the Government of the Maldive Islands, made a general economic survey of the islands. The economy of the country is almost entirely dependent on fishing. The main source of foreign aid is the United Kingdom.

*   *   *   *

The *Principality of Liechtenstein,* wedged between Austria and Switzerland, tried without success to become a member of the League of Nations. It did not apply to the United Nations, but is a party to the International Court of Justice and a member of some specialized agencies (UPU, ITU, IAEA).

The Principality is a constitutional monarchy. It has no army and only a small police force, which was recently increased from 21 to 28. Liechtenstein has used the Swiss currency since 1921, and since 1924 has been united with Switzerland in a customs union. There is complete accord between the two countries with respect to imports and exports. The mail and telegraph are administered by Switzerland. Liechtenstein has been represented by Switzerland since 1919 in all foreign affairs. Its only chargé d'affaires resides in Bern.

It has been suggested recently that the Swiss delegation to some international bodies (e.g., the Consultative Assembly of the Council of Europe) might in the future include a representative of Liechtenstein. Many international concerns have offices in the state, partly because of the low corporation taxes and partly because of the minimum investment requirements.

The present Prince lives in Liechtenstein, although his predecessors lived in Vienna. The Prince is one of the few, if not the only, Head of State to receive no salary. He is one of the wealthiest men in Europe, and his family has a fabulous art collection which is considered by many inhabitants of Liechtenstein as a national treasure, although it is the ruling family's private property.

*   *   *   *

Western Samoa, a former German protectorate in the Pacific and a League of Nations Mandated territory, then a United Nations Trust Territory, under New Zealand administration, attained independence in

1962 after a plebiscite supervised by the United Nations.

Under article 5 of the Treaty of Friendship of 1 August 1962, the Government of New Zealand must, for as long as the Government of Western Samoa wishes, and in such manner as will in no way impair the right of the Government of Western Samoa to formulate its own foreign policies, assist the Government of Western Samoa in the conduct of its international relations. When requested, New Zealand acts as the channel for communications between the Government of Western Samoa and other governments and international organizations.[20] Where permissable and appropriate, New Zealand, when requested, undertakes the representation of the Government of Western Samoa at any international conference at which Western Samoa is entitled to be represented; when requested New Zealand also supplies Western Samoa with information on international affairs and undertakes the diplomatic protection of nationals of Western Samoa in other countries, and performs consular functions on their behalf.

Article 6 provides that either Government may at any time give the other Government written notice of its desire to terminate the agreement.

In the exchange of letters of 8 March 1963, it was agreed that when the Government of Western Samoa wishes to deal directly on an official basis with one or more governments or organizations outside the South Pacific area, it will notify the New Zealand Government, and the agreement will then cease to apply in the cases and to the extent so notified. In matters of negotiations for aid or technical assistance or in routine matters, Western Samoa may decide to communicate directly with governments or international organizations, provided that the Government of New Zealand is kept informed of the cases where the Government of Western Samoa maintains this direct communication.

Liaison with New Zealand is maintained by the New Zealand High Commissioner in Apia, who is the only diplomatic representative accredited to the Government of Western Samoa.

Western Samoa chose not to become a Member of the United Nations, but is a member of WHO and ECAFE. It is also a member of the South Pacific Commission. The Western Samoan Government has taken no decision as to whether it wishes to apply to become a member of the Commonwealth, but New Zealand law continues to operate as if the new state were part of Her Majesty's dominions.

It is unlikely in the foreseeable future that Western Samoa and American Samoa will unite, or even co-operate more closely. Western

[20] In an exchange of letters dated 8 March 1963, it is agreed that the Government of New Zealand will act as the official channel of communication between the Government of Western Samoa and the governments of all countries situated outside the immediate area of the South Pacific Islands, and between the Government of Western Samoa and all international organizations having their headquarters outside that area.

Samoan society, organized on the *matai* system, is conservative and not too open to non-Samoan ideas. American Samoa, on the contrary, is interested in the American way of life. There is also a great disparity in resources, American Samoa being now much more affluent than its neighbour.

B. CONDUCT OF FOREIGN RELATIONS

The states of today do not claim absolute independence and complete economic viability as the main attributes of sovereignty and nationhood. The interdependence of states is widely accepted, and many states have joined together in different forms of unions, surrendering their prerogatives in areas previously protected jealously from any outside interference. But in the two areas of defence and foreign relations states still endeavour to retain their freedom of action and are loath to entrust decision-making and execution to any other state or supra-national organization. This is understandable, since the surviving test of independence relates to the conduct of foreign affairs and the responsicility for defence. Even when dependent territories attain complete self-government, administering Powers retain authority over defence and foreign relations. One crucial test for a territory which becomes independent is whether it could conduct its foreign relations through its own administrative and diplomatic agencies. As such, the problem of the conduct of foreign relations is of particular importance to small states and territories, and obviously the new states are concerned with the functional and substantive aspects of this question.

The conduct of foreign relations today is very different from traditional methods of diplomacy. Especially smaller countries, the emphasis has shifted from bilateral to multilateral diplomacy, which is carried out largely in the international arena through representation at international organizations. The subjects which come up for discussion have increased in range and variety, a direct result of extended state activities in such fields as trade, commerce and others hitherto carried out through private channels.

For a state to conduct foreign relations through the bilateral and multilateral agencies, it needs an adequately organized ministry with a fully trained foreign service. The conduct of foreign relations includes the process of formulating a coherent foreign policy and executing it. Admittedly, the responsibility for making policy decisions rests primarily, though not exclusively, with the foreign ministry. However, more general questions and formulations of guidelines are vested in the government of the country as a whole. Parliament or other legislative bodies also play an important rôle. Foreign policy has to be subordinated to other over-riding interests of the state. In all the small states, particularly, foreign policy decisions must take problems of development and trade into consideration.

In examining whether the small states and territories have the resources and capabilities, it will be useful to consider the experience of comparable small states which have tackled these problems successfully. Some of these older small states have been members of the United Nations or other specialized agencies for many years. They have also established and maintained bilateral relations with many countries.[21] In this task they have had to face various difficulties common to larger countries, especially in the early stages of the organization and build-up of their ministries of foreign affairs and other related mechanisms. Some of these difficulties continue to vex the bigger states as well. It can be assumed that the new small states and territories will have to pass through these stages of growth. It would be unrealistic to minimize the difficulties involved in building up the paraphernalia for foreign policy-making, including separate ministries or departments, a permanent staff and the co-ordination of activities with other departments in the government. Division of responsibility between the various branches of the government and public accountability are only some of the more prominent aspects.

Having devised this machinery, a new state has to create a cadre of foreign service officials. Diplomatic and consular officials will have to be recruited, trained and equipped for the diverse duties they are called upon to perform. There is a need also for a vast body of the clerks, security officials, cypher operators and minor officials who form the backbone of an embassy or consulate. According to the latest literature, almost all governments still face difficulties in this area. For the smaller states and territories, obstacles will be greater, particularly because of limited resources, which are often obtained from the former administering authority or a sympathetic international organization. A more complicated problem is the creation of traditions and safeguards for the control

[21] A random sample of small and medium countries with representatives accredited to foreign countries and who receive embassies and legations from other countries throws much light on the mechanism of the conduct of foreign relations.

Country	Number of representatives abroad	Number of foreign representatives in the country
Cyprus	14	34
Iceland	8	NA
Luxembourg	9	77
Kenya	8	39
Malta	5	22
Sierra Leone	9	21
Tanzania	11	46
Trinidad and Tobago	6	22
Uganda	8	27
Yemen	13	NA
Zambia	9	23

and supervision of the foreign service officials who become, even in new states, members of a privileged government department. Even though in theory the foreign service officers take instructions from the home government, in practice they often possess considerable leeway to make decisions which will have serious consequences for the lives of all the people of the country. There have been instances where diplomatic officials have committed their government to positions which the government was not willing to honour. The right balance between initiative and obedience is a difficult one to achieve, and small states will certainly need a long time to foster and fortify such traditions.

Fortunately, some of the small territories which had been governed by foreign powers, had acquired some experience and created the nucleus of machinery for conducting foreign relations through their own nationals even before attaining independence. This pre-independence experience has been diverse, ranging from the membership[22] of colonial units in international organizations to the trading activities of a minor consular or commercial official. Hence many of the small territories are not total strangers to the craft of diplomacy and the art of negotiation. Some of the difficulties of bilateral diplomacy are solved by making special arrangements, such as the handling of routine matters through representatives of other countries. Similarly, Western Samoa has by agreement entrusted the Government of New Zealand to look after its foreign interests. In the case of the Cook Islands also, New Zealand has assumed responsibility for conducting foreign relations.

It is interesting to note, however, that this delegation of powers in foreign affairs is not always absolute. In the case of Tonga, where the United Kingdom is the protecting power responsible for external relations, the Government has the right to negotiate directly with neighbouring Pacific Islands.[23] In the case of Western Samoa, the Government can unilaterally end this delegation of powers to New Zealand, either completely or only with regard to some countries or international organization.[24]

But some of these problems of bilateral foreign relations are reduced or obviated by the growth of multilateral diplomacy or the conduct of foreign relations through membership in international organizations. At the United Nations, each small state is in constant touch with more than one hundred and twenty states. Very often the communications between

[22] A number of non-independent states have been and are members of international organizations. India was a member of the League of Nations and the United Nations before becoming independent. At present, Bahrein and Qatar are associate members of FAO, UNESCO, WHO, UPU, ITU and WMO, which include many territories, small and big, considered as Non-Self-Governing Territories by the United Nations.

[23] See p. 98.
[24] See p. 110.

capitals A and B, through their representatives at New York or Geneva, is faster than direct communications between the two capitals. Even large countries still find it necessary and useful to conduct their foreign relations at the United Nations. The efforts and expenses involved are less, and maximum objectives are achieved at minimum cost. The United Nations has developed as the focus of bilateral foreign relations because it is an instrument for negotiations among, and to some extent for, governments. The many facilities provided at the headquarters of international agencies make it possible for small and big states to utilize these facilities. For the small states, it is an easy way of concentrating all foreign relations activities in one place. They are able to avoid, if necessary, the cumbersome operation of a wide and costly network of foreign posts and offices. Some facilities, of course, especially in trade matters, may have to be established in the countries directly. But the main activities which fall under the category of foreign relations can be conducted through a central office located at the Headquarters of the United Nations or other international organizations. These functions can be performed even if the small state is not a member of the international organization concerned. Perhaps in the future the small states, members and non-members of international organizations will solve many of their foreign relations problems through a centrally organized office at the most suitable international headquarters. There is evidence to believe that some states have already adopted such a practical approach.

C. PARTICIPATION OF VERY SMALL STATES AND TERRITORIES IN INTER-
   NATIONAL AND REGIONAL ORGANIZATIONS

I. THE LEAGUE OF NATIONS

None of the forty-two original Members of the League was small enough to be considered a mini-state.

Article 1, paragraph 2, of the Covenant of the League provided that

Any fully self-governing State, Dominion or Colony not named in the Annex may become a Member of the League if its admission is agreed to by two thirds of the Assembly, provided that it shall give effective guarantees of its sincere intention to observe its international obligations, and shall accept such regulations as may be prescribed by the League in regard to its military, naval and air forces and armaments.

The League twice rejected the idea of automatic membership of any state, for the sake of universality. In 1920-1921, it did not adopt an Argentinian proposal to the effect "that all sovereign States recognized by the Community of Nations be admitted to join the League of Nations in such a manner that, if they do not become Members of the League, this can only be the result of a voluntary decision on their part."[25] In 1938,

[25] *League of Nations, Second Assembly* 1921. Report of Committee I, p. 135.

the idea of universality was again rejected.[26]

Instead, the first Assembly formulated certain questions to be examined in relation to each new application for admission.[27]

(a) Is the application for admission to the League in order?

(b) Is the Government recognized *de jure* or *de facto* and by which States?

(c) Does the country possess a stable government and settled frontiers? What are its size and population?

(d) Is the country fully self-governing?

(e) What has been the conduct of the Government including both acts and assurances with regard to (i) its international obligations (ii) the prescriptions of the League as to armaments?

In the very early days of the League of Nations, a number of mini-states filed applications for membership: San Marino (23 April 1919); Iceland (2 July 1919); Luxembourg (13 February 1920); Monaco (3 May 1920) and Liechtenstein (23 July 1920).[28] The first case examined was that of Luxembourg. The report of the Fifth Committee[29] dwelt mainly on the problems posed by the neutrality of Luxembourg. It also contains one paragraph to the effect that

> the small extent of its territory and its limited population were the object of a discussion in the Committee and some members wondered whether circumstances of this kind ought not to be considered as obstacles to the admission of certain states.

But in the Plenary,[30] the Rapporteur stressed that

> the Grand Duchy of Luxembourg is an ancient state, which governs itself freely, and whose frontiers are clearly determined. She is recognized by all civilised states and has always scrupulously carried out her international obligations. From every point of view, Luxembourg is worthy to enter the League of Nations.

On 16 December 1920, the request of Luxembourg for admission was granted by 38 votes without opposition.

The request of Liechenstein came up the following day. The Fifth Committee concluded[31] that

> There can be no doubt that juridically the Principality of Liechtenstein is a sovereign state, but by reason of her limited

[26] *League of Nations*, Report of the Special Committee set up to study the application of the Principles of the Covenant, A.7. 1938 VII, pp. 41-90; Question of the universality of the League.

[27] *League of Nations, First Assembly*, Committee meetings, Vol. II. p. 159.

[28] *League of Nations, Official Journal*, July-August 1920, pp. 264-267 and 300.

[29] *First Assembly—Plenary meetings*, Annex E, p. 610.

[30] *First Assembly—Plenary meetings*, pp. 585-586.

[31] *First Assembly—Plenary meetings*, Annex C, p. 667.

area, small population and her geographical position, she has chosen to depute to others some of the attributes of sovereignty. For instance, she has contracted with other Powers for the control of her customs, the administration of her Posts, Telegraph and Telephone Services, for the diplomatic representation of her subjects in foreign countries other than Switzerland and Austria, for final decision in certain judicial cases. Liechtenstein has no army. For the above reasons we are of the opinion that the Principality of Liechtenstein could not discharge all the international obligations which would be imposed on her by the Covenant.

In the Plenary meeting,[32] on 17 December 1920, the admission of Liechtenstein was rejected by 28 votes to 1 (Switzerland). Switzerland stated that

if the Assembly were not disposed to admit Liechtenstein to full membership of the League, yet it was of great importance that in some way or another small states should be brought within the comity of the nations of the world and that it was not fair, because a state was very small, to leave it altogether outside the organisations of the nations of the world.

Therefore, the Swiss representative suggested that

Switzerland might be allowed, as it were, to represent Liechtenstein in the Assembly.[33]

Instead, the Assembly adopted the recommendation proposed by the Committee that

the Special Committee appointed by the Council of the League of Nations to consider proposals with reference to amendments to the Covenant, should also consider whether and in what manner it would be possible to attach to the League of Nations sovereign states which, by reason of their small size, cannot be admitted as ordinary members.[34]

In the meantime, Monaco had withdrawn its application, and San Marino failed to respond to the Secretary-General's request for information to support its application. Similarly, no further action was taken on the application of Iceland.

The following year (1921), a sub-committee presented a report on the "Position of Small States."[35] The sub-committee stated that

it was of the opinion that it was very desirable for the development of the League of Nations that the latter should, as soon as possible, include all those States which have fulfilled the

[32] *First Assembly—Plenary meetings*, Annex C, p. 652.
[33] *First Assembly—Plenary meetings*, p. 643.
[34] *First Assembly—Plenary meetings*, p. 652.
[35] *Second Assembly—Plenary meetings*, pp. 685-686.

conditions laid down in Article 1 of the Covenant, and which wish to join the League. This principle applies equally, although with less importance, to States of a very small area, since every State constitutes a moral entity whose susceptibilities should be respected. Moreover, the true object of the League, the development of co-operation among nations, with a view to guaranteeing peace and security, would be more readily attained if a certain class of States, even States of secondary importance, were not excluded.

However, the decision taken about Liechtenstein precluded the possibility of admitting small states as ordinary members. Three possibilities were envisaged:

(a) either small states might be "associated" and given a right of full representation without a vote; or

(b) they might be allowed to be "represented" by some other state which was already a member of the League; or

(c) a third system, that of "limited participation," might be employed. This system would allow states of this kind to enjoy all the privileges of ordinary members, but the exercise of these privileges would be limited exclusively to cases in which their own interests were involved. Their "association" would be restricted to taking part in debates or in votes to the extent that a majority of the Assembly might decide that the national interests of these states were involved therein.

None of these solutions found favour in the Committee, and in addition it was noted that all three systems would appear to necessitate an amendment to the Covenant. Therefore, after discussion in the First Committee[36] and in the Plenary,[37] it was decided, on 4 October 1921, to adopt the following conclusions:

As regards those sovereign States which, on account of their small size, cannot aspire to the status of ordinary Members of the League of Nations, although they might desire to benefit from the institutions of the League in a great many respects;

In view of the difficulty of laying down in advance the conditions for the admission of these States, the different situations of which might necessitate different conditions;

And, in view of the possibility of associating immediately, to a great extent, the interested States in the work of the Assembly, without giving them membership;

The Committee considers it preferable to await the result of experience in this collaboration, before expressing an opinion upon the methods by which they might be admitted to the League.

There is no trace of a further assessment of the "results of experience in this collaboration" (i.e., the possibility for small states of participating in specific conferences convoked by the League, of acceding

[36] Second Assembly—First Committee, pp. 17-21.
[37] Second Assembly—Plenary meetings, pp. 818-820.

to international conventions, having their treaties registered, etc.). And no further systematic consideration seems to have been given by the League of Nations to the problem of small states.

In a 1938 report to the Assembly on the application of the principles of the Covenant, the idea of some form of associate membership was again considered and rejected on the ground that it would give rise to more difficulties than it would solve.[38]

However, the League reaffirmed that it had been its consistent policy to invite the collaboration of non-member states in the work of the League. This practice was widely followed, particularly in technical fields.[39]

The League of Nations made no formal provision for observers from non-member countries.

II. THE UNITED NATIONS

In the United Nations, the question of the participation of small states raised no major difficulty in the early days of the Organization. Luxembourg is an original Member. Iceland was admitted on 19 November 1946. Monaco, Liechtenstein and San Marino never applied for membership, but Monaco has had an Observer Mission at the United Nations since 1956. Liechtenstein and San Marino are both parties to the Statute of the International Court of Justice.

In 1949, when the Security Council debated the application of Liechtenstein to become a party to that Statute, two members of the Security Council (Union of Soviet Socialist Republics and Ukrainian SSR) argued that Liechtenstein, having no army, currency, or postal or telegraph administration of its own and conducting its foreign affairs through Switzerland, was not really sovereign and therefore should not be entitled to become a party to the Statute. However, it is interesting to note that in the Security Council,[40] the delegate of the Ukrainian SSR specifically excluded any consideration of size from his assessment of the case:

> From the point of view of principle, we have always taken the stand that a state, however small, has the same rights as a large state in the matter of joining the United Nations or becoming a party to the Statute of the International Court of Justice. The question of whether a given state has a large territory or a small one, or whether it has a large population or not, is of no consequence to us.

[38] Report of the Special Committee set up to study the application of the Principles of the Covenant, A.7. 1938. VII, pp. 58-59.

[39] Memorandum by the Secretariat of the League of Nations on the Relations of the League with Non-Member States, C.368.M.250.1937.VII.

[40] SCOR, S/PV.432. The vote in the Security Council was 9 in favour, 2 abstentions.

The Union of Soviet Socialist Republics and the Ukrainian SSR abstained in the vote in the Security Council, and subsequently the General Assembly, after discussion in the Sixth Committee,[41] voted in favour of Liechtenstein's application.[42]

In 1953, San Marino also applied to become a party to the Statute of the International Court of Justice. It was approved by the Security Council,[43] upon the report of the Committee of experts and by the General Assembly,[44] without debate.

In subsequent years, a number of states with a population under one million have been admitted to membership in the United Nations without any objection: Congo (Brazzaville), Cyprus and Gabon in 1960; Trinidad and Tobago in 1962; Kuwait in 1963; Malta in 1964; The Gambia and the Maldive Islands in 1964; Guyana, Botswana, Lesotho and Barbados in 1966; Mauritius, Equatorial Guinea and Swaziland in 1968; Fiji in 1970.

The first application of Kuwait in 1961 was vetoed in the Security Council by the Union of Soviet Socialist Republics.[45] It was not a question of size, but of the fact that Iraq had a claim on that territory. Further, the USSR did not consider that Kuwait had really become independent from the United Kingdom on 19 June 1961, when the Protectorate agreement of 23 January 1899 was terminated. However, Iraq did mention size as an additional argument. In describing Kuwait to the General Assembly, the Foreign Minister of Iraq questioned whether "it was possible to declare a number of oil wells a State."[46] Iraq's representative to the Security Council, who had asked to participate in the debate without voting, said that Kuwait was not a state but "a small town outside the confines of which there exists no settled population, but roaming nomads; and yet we are asked to admit this overgrown village to membership of the United Nations."[47] However, all members of the Security Council except the Union of Soviet Socialist Republics expressed the view that Kuwait was an independent sovereign state, recognized by a majority of Member States, and already a member of various specialized

[41] GAOR, Fourth session, A/C.6/SR.174, 26 October 1949. The vote in the Sixth Committee was 42 in favour, 4 against, 1 abstention.

[42] GAOR, Fourth session, A/PV.262 and General Assembly resolutions 363 (IV) of 1 December 1949. The vote in the plenary was 40 in favour, 2 against, 2 abstentions.

[43] SCOR, S/PV.645, 3 December 1953. The vote in the Security Council was 10 in favour, 1 abstention.

[44] GAOR, Eighth session. A/PV.471 and General Assembly resolution 806 (VIII) of 9 December 1953. The vote in the plenary was 51 in favour, 5 abstentions.

[45] SCOR, S/PV.984-5, 30 November 1961. The vote in the Security Council was 10 in favour, 1 against.

[46] GAOR, Sixteenth session, A/PV.1028, 6 October 1961.

[47] SCOR, S/PV.984, 30 November 1961.

agencies and the League of Arab States. A year and a half later, Kuwait received unanimous support in the Security Council[48] and was admitted by the General Assembly by acclamation.[49]

The application of the Maldive Islands was unanimously supported in the Security Council on 20 September 1965. The representative of the United Kingdom stated: "The population of the islands is just short of 100,000 people, and the widely scattered islands in the past have usually been remote from the main currents of world events. But, comparatively small in population and in its total areas, as the Maldives are, the application now before us could not be supported by better qualifications."[50] The French representative,[51] while supporting the admission of the Maldive Islands, pointed out "that in view of the responsibilities which are incumbent upon us under rule 60 of the provisional rules of procedure of the Security Council, the Security Council should not lose sight of the provisions of rule 59.[52] That rules provides for a procedure which offers supplementary possibilities for reflection and judgment, from which it seems essential for us to benefit from now on if we do not wish to see the long-range effectiveness of the Organization diminish."

The representative of the United States of America, while supporting the admission of the Maldive Islands to the United Nations, stated:

> We cannot help but note in this connexion a basic problem which will confront the United Nations in the future. There are many small entities in the world today moving steadily towards some form of independence. We are in sympathy with their aspirations and applaud this development. However, the Charter provides that applicants for United Nations membership must not be only willing but also able to carry out their Charter obligations. The drafters of the Charter were not unmindful of the existence then of some very small states whose resources would simply not permit them to contribute to the work of the Organization, however much they might wish to do so. Today, many of the small emerging entities, however willing, probably do not have the human or economic resources at this stage to meet this second criterion. We would therefore urge that Council members and

[48] *Ibid..* S/PV.1034, 7 May 1963.
[49] GAOR, Fourth special session, A/PV.1203, 14 May 1963.
[50] SCOR, S/PV.1243, 20 September 1965.
[51] *Ibid.*
[52] Rule 60 provides that "the Security Council shall decide whether in its judgment, the applicant is a peace-loving state and is able and willing to carry out the obligations contained in the Charter, and accordingly whether to recommed the applicant state for membership." Rule 59 states that "unless the Security Council decides otherwise, the application for membership shall be referred by the President to a committee of the Security Council upon which each member of the Security Council shall be represented."

other United Nations Members give early and careful consideration to this problem in an effort to arrive at some agreed standards, some lower limits, to be applied in the case of future applicants for United Nations membership. The original members of the Security Council evidently had this complex of problems in mind when they provided, in rule 59 of the provisional rules of procedures, for a Special Committee of the Council to examine membership applications and to report its conclusions to the Council. The Council may wish, as the representative of France has suggested, to avail itself of this procedure, both in reviewing general problems and in examining future applications for membership concerning which some of these considerations might arise. We do not for a moment suggest the exclusion of small new States from the family of nations; on the contrary, we believe we must develop for them some accommodation that will permit their close association with the United Nations and its broad range of activities. This is another facet of the problem that we think demands early and careful consideration.[53]

On 14 October 1966, when the Security Council was examining the unanimously supported admission of Botswana and Lesotho to the United Nations, the representative of Argentina stated:

The honour represented by being in the Organization goes hand in hand with an onerous responsibility. The duties are many; the commitments unavoidable. That is why the Argentine Government believes that perhaps we ought not to consider rule 58 of the provisional rules of procedure of the Security Council as a mere formality.[54] I hasten to state that we are not considering this rule from the point of view of excluding anyone, but, rather, with a desire truly to interpret our fundamental document, the Charter of the United Nations, and to adhere as closely as possible to the spirit underlying its words. It is for that reason that we feel it only appropriate to recall what was said by the representatives of France and the United States at the meeting of 20 September 1965 of the Security Council with reference to rule 59 of the provisional rules of procedure, specifically when it mentions a committee of the Security Council charged with examining applications for membership. We believe their suggestions warrant consideration, particularly since it is a well known fact that new territories, some of them extremely small and with very limited resources, will in the near future accede to independence.[55]

The Secretary-General raised the question of the mini-states twice in his annual reports. In 1965, he stated:

[53] SCOR, S/PV.1243, 20 September 1965.

[54] Rule 58: "Any state which desires to become a Member of the United Nations shall submit an application to the Security Council. This application shall contain a declaration made in a formal instrument that it accepts the obligations contained in the Charter."

[55] SCOR, S/PV.1306, 14 October 1966.

A different aspect of the question of the extent of participation by countries in organized international activities is raised by the recent phenomenon of the emergence of exceptionally small new States. Their limited size and resources can pose a difficult problem as to the rôle they should try to play in international life. In one or two cases, such States have decided to restrict their membership to one or more of the specialized agencies, so that they may at any rate receive the fullest possible assistance from the United Nations system in advancing their economic and social development. I believe that the time has come when Member States may wish to examine more closely the criteria for the admission of new Members in the light of the long-term implications of the present trends.[56]

In 1967, he made a fuller statement on the same subject:[57]

I believe it is necessary to note that, while universality of membership is most desirable, like all concepts it has its limitations and the line has to be drawn somewhere. Universality, as such, is not mentioned in the Charter, although suggestions to this effect were made, but not adopted, at San Francisco, and the Charter itself foresees limitations on United Nations membership. Under Article 4 of the Charter not only must a State be peace-loving, but it must also, in the judgment of the Organization, be able and willing to carry out the obligations contained in the Charter.

In making this observation, I have in mind those States which have been referred to as 'micro-States,' entities which are exceptionally small in area, population and human and economic resources, and which are now emerging as independent States. For example, the Trust Territory of Nauru, which is expected to attain independence in the immediate future, has an area of 8.25 square miles and an indigenous population of about 3,000, while Pitcairn Island is only 1.75 square miles in extent and has a population of eighty-eight.

It is, of course, perfectly legitimate that even the smallest territories, through the exercise of their right to self-determination, should attain independence as a result of the effective application of General Assembly resolution 1514 (XV) on the granting of independence to colonial countries and peoples. However, it appears desirable that a distinction be made between the right to independence and the question of full membership in the United Nations. Such membership may, on the one hand, impose obligations which are too onerous for the 'micro-States' and, on the other hand, may lead to a weakening of the United Nations itself.

I would suggest that it may be opportune for the competent organs to undertake a thorough and comprehensive study of the criteria for membership in the United Nations, with a view to laying down the necessary limitations on full membership while

[56] Document A/6001/Add.1. p. 2.
[57] Document A/6701/Add.1, paras. 162-1 6.

also defining other forms of association which would benefit both the 'micro-States' and the United Nations. I fully realize that a suggestion of this nature involves considerable political difficulties, but if it can be successfully undertaken it will be very much in the interests both of the United Nations and of the 'micro-States' themselves. There are already one or two cases where the States concerned have realized that their best interests, for the time being at least, rest in restricting themselves to membership in certain specialized agencies, so that they can benefit fully from the United Nations system in advancing their economic and social development without having to assume the heavy financial and other responsibilities involved in United Nations membership. The League of Nations had to face the same issue over the question of the admission of certain European States which were then referred to as 'Lilliputian' States. Although the League of Nations was unable to define exact criteria, it prevented in due course the entry of the 'Lilliputian' States.

As already mentioned, a necessary corollary to the establishment of criteria on admission to full membership is the definition of other forms of association for 'micro-States' which would not qualify for full membership. As members of the international community, such States are entitled to expect that their security and territorial integrity should be guaranteed and to participate to the full in international assistance for economic and social development. Even without Charter amendment, there are various forms of association, other than full membership, which are available, such as access to the International Court of Justice and membership in the relevant United Nations regional economic commissions. Membership in the specialized agencies also provides an opportunity for access to the benefits provided by the United Nations Development Programme and for invitations to United Nations conferences. In addition to participation along the foregoing lines, 'micro-States' should also be permitted to establish permanent observer missions at United Nations Headquarters and at the United Nations Office at Geneva, if they so wish, as is already the case in one or two instances. Measures of this nature would permit the 'micro-States' to benefit fully from the United Nations system without straining their resources and potential through assuming the full burdens of United Nations membership which they are not, through lack of human and economic resources, in a position to assume.

On 13 December 1967, the Permanent Representative of the United States of America addressed a letter[58] to the President of the Security Council, in which he stated:

It is our belief that examination of the considerations presented by the Secretary-General is most likely to be fruitful if it

[58] Document S/8296.

is made in terms of general principles and procedures. Inasmuch as no applications for membership are now pending in the Security Council, we believe the time may be appropriate for considering the suggestions that have been put forward.

Members of the Council will recall that rule 59 requires that in the absence of a contrary decision by the Security Council, applications for membership be referred by the President to the Committee on the Admission of New Members. Although the Committee on Membership has in fact been inactive for some time, it is a standing committee under the rules, on which all members of the Council are represented.

The United States believes that the Security Council could usefully and appropriately seek the assistance and advice of this Committee in examining the issues outlined by the Secretary-General with a view to providing the members and the Security Council with appropriate information and advice. We would accordingly request that as President of the Council you consult the members about the possibility of reconvening the Committee for such a purpose.

Apparently, nothing happened for six months, after which time a meeting of the Committee on the Admission of New Members was scheduled for 27 June 1968 (the month during which the representative of the United States of America was President of the Council). The meeting was cancelled, however, and no new date set. It seems that there is a certain reluctance in various quarters to grapple with the question of membership criteria.[59] It may be that rather than examine the question of admission in terms of general principles and procedure as suggested by the United States of America, most members find it easier and less embarrassing to continue to examine each application individually on its own merits.

On 14 July 1969 the Representative of the United States of America revived the issue and requested an early meeting of the Security Council and of its Committee on the Admission of New Members on the question of micro-states.[60] On 19 August 1969 the United States Representative stated that the Security Council should request the Secretary-General to place the question of associate membership before the General Assembly, and that it establish an expert committee of the Security Council to study this question and to report its recommendations to the Security Council, which in due course should transmit these recommendations to the General Assembly at its 24th session.[61]

[59] In the Introduction to his Annual Report, 1967-68 (document A/7201/Add.1, para. 172), the Secretary-General remarks: "I can well understand the reluctance of the principal organs to grapple with this problem [of the micro-states], but I believe it is a problem that does require urgent attention."

[60] S/9327.

[61] S/9397.

The Security Council considered the matter on 27 and 29 August 1969.[62] It had received a formal draft resolution from the United States,[63] as follows:

> The Security Council,
>
> Bearing in mind that membership in the United Nations is open to all peace-loving States which accept the obligations contained in the Charter and which are able and willing to carry out these obligations;
>
> Further bearing in mind the increasing emergence of States so small that they would be unable to carry out the obligations of full membership,
>
> Desirous of ensuring that all such States should nevertheless be able to associate themselves with the United Nations in order to further the principles and purposes of the Organization and derive benefits from such association,
>
> Requests the Secretary-General to inscribe on the provisional agenda of the 24th session of the General Assembly an item entitled "Creation of a Category of Associate Membership."

The Representative of the United States argued that there was now "a brief opportunity to act on the basis of general principles, because again at this moment no applications for membership lie before the Security Council." He also suggested that the Security Council refer the problem for study to a Committee of Experts. "This Committee should report the results of its study and its recommendations to the Council within two months, which would bring us to the beginning of November (1969) in time for the Council in turn to make recommendations to the General Assembly during the 24th session."

All members of the Security Council agreed that there was a micro-state problem and a problem of associate membership, and that it was desirable to establish a committee of experts to study them. But many stressed that the matter was complex and delicate, and that it would be premature for the Security Council to adopt immediately a request for the inscription of the question of associate membership on the agenda of the General Assembly. "There is no reason for such a haste," said the Representative of the Union of Soviet Socialist Republics. "I would not wish to accept immediately the terms of the draft resolution which has been suggested," said the Representative of the United Kingdom. "The Security Council must take into account the fact that the creation of a particular status, if agreed to, would necessarily lead to a substantive modification of the Charter. Consequently my delegation considers it desirable that prior to any other decision, the Security Council should entrust to a committee of experts of the Council the task of undertaking a

[62] S/PV.1505-1506.
[63] S/9414.

thorough study of this important question," said the Representative of France.

After two days of debate the Security Council took no action on the draft proposed by the United States, but decided to set up a committee of experts, consisting of all members of the Security Council, "to study the question which was examined at the 1505th and 1506th meetings of the Security Council."

The Committee of Experts held four closed meetings in September, October and November 1969. As of the end of 1969, it had not completed its task, nor submitted a report to the Security Council. The question of associate membership was never inscribed on the agenda of the 24th session of the General Assembly.

Many political observers express scepticism as to the practical results of the work of the Committee of Experts of the Security Council on the questions of micro-states and associate membership.

It is unlikely that smallness of population *per se* or area will ever be considered a factor against admission. Article 4 of the Charter reads:

> Membership in the United Nations is open to all other[64] peace-loving states which accept the obligations contained in the present Charter and in the judgment of the Organization are able and willing to carry out these obligations.

Of course, one might theoretically create arbitrary minimum standards of size, such as population or a combination of population, area and economic indicators (GNP, *per capita* income, government revenue and expenditures or foreign trade). The possibility of agreeing on a single formula for all applicants is remote.

Objections not based directly on size, but in fact linked to it, can be derived from two provisions in Article 4:

(a) The country applying for admission must be a *state*.

(b) It must be judged by the United Nations as *able* to carry out the obligations contained in the Charter.

A. *A state*

Under traditional international law, it has been commonly assumed that four criteria must be met before an entity can be said to be a state. It should possess (a) a permanent population, (b) a defined territory, (c) a government, (d) the capacity to enter into relations with other states.[65]

Using similar criteria, it has been contended that to be termed a state, a community should in fact govern its own territory, maintain a reasonable degree of law and order and reasonable security for foreigners

---

[64] Than original Members of the United Nations.

[65] Rosalyn Higgins, *The Development of International Law through the Political Organs of the United Nations*, 1963; Chap. I "The concept of statehood in United Nations practice."

legitimately present, and be able to exchange goods and services.[66]

These requirements presumably will not present insurmountable obstacles to mini-states seeking acceptance as states by the United Nations. It is most unlikely that islands in the Pacific without permanent populations or recently emerged uninhabited islands will apply for membership. The question of what would happen to a mini-Member whose entire population was leaving its territory is theoretical and hypothetical.[67]

Conflicting claims may exist over certain territories or their boundaries. Iraq's claims to Kuwait's territory did not prevent Kuwait's accession to membership. Conflicting claims exist over certain mini-territories, such as the claim of Morocco against Spain over Ifni;[68] Morocco and Mauritania against Spain over Spanish Sahara; Argentina against the United Kingdom over the Falkland (Malvina) Islands; Guatemala against the United Kingdom over British Honduras (Belize); Spain against the United Kingdom over Gibraltar. If and when these territories become independent and apply for membership, difficulties may arise, if some kind of a decision has not previously been taken on these claims, with United Nations endorsement.

It is doubtful that the Security Council or the General Assembly will ever embark upon a discussion on the definition of state, and more particularly on the question of when limitations of size precludes application of the concept of state.

The criterion which may give rise to controversies in certain cases is the problem of adequacy of independence and sovereignty which a territory must possess.

International law doctrine is not quite clear on the criteria of legal and actual independence, which are questions of degree as well as fact. It has been said that certain states have been admitted to the United Nations whose true independence is questionable. This illustrates the difficulty of ascertaining the facts needed to judge whether a territory is

---

[66] *Seventeenth Report of the Commission to Study the Organization of Peace.* U.G. Whitaker, "Reconciling power and sovereignty."

[67] A curious example of a particularly difficult situation of a mini-territory without a permanent population is the request of the Banabans of Ocean Island, in the Gilbert and Ellice Islands Colony, for the constitution of a separate and independent state (see document A/AC.109/SR.606, 11 June 1968). The 2,000 Banabans, who are the owners and former inhabitants of the phosphate Ocean Island, were all moved after World War II 1,200 miles to the west to Rabi Island, which is part of Fiji. The Banabans continue to receive royalties for the phosphates extracted from Ocean Island. However, on Ocean Island there is only one Banaban left (the labour force comes from other islands). It appears now that the Banabans want to secede from the Gilbert and Ellice Islands Colony and claim independence for their island, which they have not inhabited for over twenty years.

[68] On 4 January 1969, Spain transferred Ifni to Morocco.

really independent and sovereign.[69] It has been argued that because of arrangements made by a small state, delegating some of its prerogatives to other countries, its sovereignty and independence are no longer sufficiently intact, and that therefore it cannot be accepted as a state Member of the Organization. This was the case made by the majority against Liechtenstein when it applied for admission to the League,[70] and again by a minority when it succeeded in becoming a party to the Statute of the International Court of Justice.[71]

Limitations on a state's ability to conclude commercial treaties or conduct its own foreign policy are mentioned as examples of restrictions on sovereignty which might jeopardize admission to the United Nations. The extent to which defence arrangements concluded between former colonial Powers and newly independent states impair the independence of the new states has also been the subject of comment in a number of cases, but even the existence of important foreign military bases on their territory has not prevented states such as Malta, Cyprus and the Maldive Islands from becoming Members of the United Nations.

B. *Ability and willingness to carry out the objectives contained in the Charter*

If a state, however small, declares formally that it is willing to carry out certain obligations, it is hardly conceivable that the Organization would not recognize this willingness. As to ability, as has been indicated above, there were cases where it was argued that a state was legally unable to carry out certain obligations for lack of complete independence. However, it is unlikely that a controversy would arise about the ability of a mini-state to settle international disputes by peaceful means, to refrain from the threat or use of force, to co-operate with the Organization in economic and social matters or to comply with decisions of the International Court of Justice. As far as supporting United Nations actions for the maintenance of peace and security, a small state might have no armed forces, but might still provide valuable bases, staging areas, landing fields, etc.[72]

The most tangible measure of ability to carry out the obligations of the Charter is the obligation to make a financial contribution to the Organization.[73]

The Committee on contributions has assessed the various Member

[69] Rosalyn Higgins, *Ibid.,* pp. 26-27.

[70] See *supra,* p. 121.

[71] See *supra,* p. 125.

[72] Patricia W. Blair, *The Ministate Dilemma,* Occasional Paper No. 6, Carnegie Endowment for International Peace, October 1967, pp. 25-26.

[73] Costa Rica withdrew from the League of Nations in 1925 on the ground that the annual contribution was beyond her means (see F. P. Walters, *A History of the League of Nations,* p. 325).

States according to capacity to pay. This is determined mainly by national income, but with reductions for certain countries which have a low *per capita* income (*per capita* contribution of any Member should not exceed the *per capita* contribution of the Member which has the highest assessment). In addition, a minimum assessment has been established at 0.04 per cent, not only for the United Nations but for FAO, UNESCO, WHO and IAEA (for other agencies the minimum percentage is slightly higher). Of the 126 Members of the United Nations, 60 are assessed at the minimum rate of 0.04 per cent. Of the 15 Member States with a population of less than one million, 13 are assessed at the minimum rate of 0.04 per cent (Kuwait is assessed at the rate of 0.07 per cent, Luxembourg at the rate of 0.05 per cent). Of the eight non-Member States contributing to the expenses of the International Court of Justice, the International Control of Narcotic Drugs, ECAFE and/or UNCTAD, four (Liechtenstein, San Marino, Monaco and the Holy See) are assessed at the rate of 0.04 per cent.

The gross appropriation for the 1967 United Nations budget was $129,236,930. The net figure is $108,671,804. The gross minimum assessment of 0.04 per cent therefore is $51,700 (net $43,500).

Participation in all United Nations agencies[74] would be as follows:

	1967 Appropriations Gross	US$ net	Minimum Contribution per cent	Net Contribution
ILO	26,523,125	22,472,398	0.11	24,720
FAO	29,637,229	24,022,294	0.04	9,609
UNESCO	33,644,288	28,985,854	0.04	11,592
ICAO	7,125,221	5,559,000	0.13	7,226
UPU	1,594,815	1,400,232	0.11	1,540
WHO	58,097,380	52,075,600	0.04	20,830
ITU	6,082,083	5,171,041	0.10	5,171
WMO	3,083,350	2,937,629	0.09	2,673
IMCO	820,766	818,066	0.24	1,963
IAEA	10,613,000	9,174,000	0.04	3,669
	178,021,627	152,616,114		88,993
UN	129,236,930	108,671,804	0.04	43,469
	307,258,197	261,288,918		132,461

Membership in the United Nations and all its agencies is therefore a relatively expensive proposition in terms of contributions only. However, it is possible that if many more mini-states were to be admitted, an attempt might be made to lower the minimum contribution rate. It is

[74] Document A/6911.

interesting to note that per capita U.N. assessment is higher for mini-states.

When The Gambia was admitted to the United Nations in 1965, reference was made to the high cost of membership. The Prime Minister, who was representing The Gambia in the General Assembly, stated:

> With my people I take pride in the thought that, without ever departing from the path of peaceful and orderly progress, The Gambia has taken its rightful place in the family of nations. But I am all humility when I reflect that, in terms of size, population and resources, The Gambia is one of the smallest countries to achieve national sovereignty and a place in the international community. This presents very special problems when a country like The Gambia finds that it is expected to contribute to the expenses of the United Nations on the basis of a minimum contribution which is out of proportion to its resources, and to join specialized agencies which intend to assess the country's contribution on the basis of the same minimum rates. This problem has been explained to the Secretary-General, and unless a solution can be found, it may well mean that my country may not be able to participate in the affairs of the United Nations to the extent which we would wish.[75]

In 1967, the representative of The Gambia reiterated this view:

> Besides living in peace and co-operating with its neighbours, my country will continue to support the United Nations. I must say, however, that effective support will depend on whether or not we shall be able to afford continued membership of this Organiza-tion. At the level at which The Gambia is assessed for contribu-tions, this is, to say the least, doubtful. We have made repeated representations, not only to this Organization, but also to the Organization of African Unity and to various Commonwealth organizations, about the rates at which The Gambia is assessed for contributions to these organizations.
>
> We strongly feel that these scales and rates are based on data and criteria which do not take into account the circumstances of small unendowed countries like The Gambia. We question the equity of applying to The Gambia a minimum rate which was fixed for countries several times larger and richer. Our representations have met with some success in the Organization of African Unity[76] and in the Commonwealth organizations of which we are mem-bers. I hope that they will be taken in good part here, thus enabling The Gambia to continue to play its part and to discharge its obligations in the comity of nations.[77]

[75] GAOR, Twentieth session, A/PV.1332, 21 September 1965.

[76] The Gambia's yearly contribution to the OAU budget was reduced from £30,000 to £4,000.

[77] GAOR, Twenty-second session, A/PV.1566, 25 September 1967.

So far, The Gambia has not felt compelled to leave the United Nations, and no consideration has been given to lowering the minimum contribution percentage.

However, The Gambia has no permanent delegation in New York; it is the only Member State to have adopted this measure of economy.

In general, small Member States have smaller delegations. Based on the official list of Permanent Missions to the United Nations in September 1968, the average number of personnel for 123[78] Members was 8.2 whereas 14[79] Member States with a population of one million or less, the average was 4.

There is no case where the United Nations considered a small Member State or prospective Member State unable to carry out its Charter obligations. The feeling of the majority in the United Nations seems to be that such an issue should be discussed only when a specific case arises. The desirability of discussing at this stage the admission of mini-states "in terms of general principles and procedures," as suggested by the United States of America in December 1967, seems, in the opinion of many Members, to be neither an urgent nor an important issue.

Among the reasons given, the following seem the most prevalent ones:

(a) The ratios among present Member States, in terms of population, area and *per capita* GNP, are already so unbalanced that a further increase caused by the admission of new mini-states would not be of great significance.

In 1965, the population ratio between India and the Maldive Islands was 483,000,000 to 98,000, or 4,928/1. The area ratio between the Union of Soviet Socialist Republics and Malta was 22,402,200 to 316, or 70,720/1. The *per capita* GNP ratio between the United States of America and Lesotho was 3,020 to 60, or 50/1.

(b) It is not likely that the United Nations would want to prevent the entry of a state whose population is as large as or larger than that of present Member States at the time of their admission. Seventeen Members of the United Nations have a population of one million or less. Of those, only Luxembourg and Iceland were independent States before 1960.

The two smallest Members in that regard are the Maldive Islands (population in 1965, year of admission: 98,000) and Iceland (population in 1946, year of admission: 132,000).[80] These precedents would open the door of the United Nations to territories with populations over

[78] Based on UN Statistical Yearbook 1966, Table 14.

[79] Not including Swaziland and Equatorial Guinea, not yet listed, and The Gambia.

[80] It may also be recalled that when Western Samoa became independent on 1 January 1962 (population at that time: 114,000), the General Assembly "expressed the hope that Western Samoa, on the attainment of

100,000, which includes approximately half the emergent territories with populations under 1,000,000 (see Table II).

(c) Some Member States, including small States, have opposed the idea of any limitation of membership based on size.[81]

(d) It is believed that a number of small territories which will become independent in the future may choose to follow the lead of Western Samoa and Nauru and not apply for membership in the United Nations.

(e) It is also believed that a number of small territories which will exercise their right to self-determination in the future may choose a status short of independence with the concurrence of the United Nations, as was the case with the Cook Islands.

Therefore, it is contended that the number of independent states with populations under 100,000 which will apply for full United Nations membership may in fact not be as large as is commonly thought.

The United Nations Charter makes no provision for restricted forms of membership, although such membership exists in some of its bodies, for instance, the Regional Economic Commissions (see below).

In 1967, Sub-Committee III of the Special Committee of Twenty-Four considered a proposal made by Iran that the Secretary-General initiate a study of arrangements under which the small territories wishing to be fully self-governing might be enabled to have available to them the status of sovereign entities associated with the United Nations.[82] No action was taken on this proposal.

In 1968, however, the Special Committee of Twenty-Four adopted a recommendation proposed by its Sub-Committee III that the Committee decide "to initiate, with the assistance of the Secretary-General, a study of the question of the small Territories in accordance with paragraph 17 of General Assembly resolution 2326 (XXII) which invited the Special Committee to pay particular attention to the small Territories and to recommend to the General Assembly the most appropriate methods and also the steps to be taken to enable the populations of those Territories to exercise fully their right to self-determination and independence."[83]

Non-Member States have some access to United Nations activities,

---

independence, will be admitted to membership in the United Nations should it so desire" (General Assembly resolution 1626 (XVI) of 18 October 1961). Western Samoa never applied for membership.

[81] The representative of Luxembourg stated, *inter alia*: ". . . But if in the future this right [of membership in the United Nations] was to be based merely on size, or size defined in terms of geographic dimensions or of population, or even by *per capita* income, we would be entering into the realm of the arbitrary, which would render valueless the fundamental principles of our Organization" (A/PV.1688, 9 October 1968).

[82] A/6700/Add.14 (Part II), para. 286.

[83] A/7200 (Part I). paras. 125-135.

either under the provisions of the Charter or under adopted practices.

Under Article 35, paragraph 2, "A state which is not a Member of the United Nations may bring to the attention of the Security Council or the General Assembly any dispute to which it is a party, if it accepts in advance, for the purposes of the dispute, the obligations of pacific settlement provided in the present Charter."

Under Article 32, ". . . any State which is not a member of the United Nations, if it is a party to a dispute under consideration by the Security Council, shall be invited to participate without vote in the discussion relating to the dispute."

Article 2, paragraph 6 (international peace and security), 50 (enforcement measures) and 93 (International Court of Justice) also contain references to non-Member States.

The practice of the Economic and Social Council and its commissions provides for extensive participation by non-Members in their activities. Also, the Assembly and its organs grant hearings to non-governmental organizations, associations and individuals. Access of petitioners to the Trusteeship Council, the Fourth Committee and the Committee of Twenty-Four has made it possible for representatives of sections of the population of dependent mini-territories to be heard in United Nations organs, before independence.

No provision is made for observers in the Charter of the United Nations or the rules of procedure of the General Assembly. In practice, however, a number of non-Member States do send observers to the United Nations and have established permanent offices at Headquarters. Among the small non-Member States maintaining permanent observers offices at Headquarters are the Holy See and Monaco. San Marino has an observer at the United Nations Office in Geneva. The Secretary-General has welcomed these observers and has given their missions every possible facility, even though their status is not yet determined.

In his Introduction to the Annual Report on the Work of the Organization 1966-1967, the Secretary-General specifically refers to the possibility that micro-states might establish permanent observer missions in New York and Geneva. In this connexion, he recalls that in spite of the fact that he has often raised the question of observers in general, "the institution is one which rests purely on practice and which has not been set on any firm legal basis through discussions and decision in the General Assembly."[84] According to present practice,[85] the facilities for observers from non-Member States are generally the same as those for distinguished visitors. The Secretariat arranges for their seating in the public gallery at meetings. All relevant unrestricted United Nations

[84] Document A/6701/Add.1, para. 167.

[85] Document ST/LEG/8, 22 August 1962, pp.236-237—Legal opinion of the Secretariat of the United Nations.

documentation is distributed to them, and their names are appended for convenience of reference to the List of Permanent Missions to the United Nations published monthly by the Secretariat. However, these observers are not entitled to diplomatic privileges and immunities, nor are they given assistance to obtain visas from the United States Government. Communications from observers and non-Member States are only distributed as documents if a request to this effect is made by a Member State.[86] They may not address meetings unless specifically invited to do so. Communications relating to the appointment of an observer are merely acknowledged, and the person appointed may be received by the Secretary-General as a matter of courtesy, but not for the purpose of presenting his credentials.

III. SPECIALIZED ORGANS OF THE UNITED NATIONS

States, which are not Members of the United Nations, are members of UNCTAD (United Nations Conference on Trade and Development) and UNIDO (United Nations Industrial Development Organization). They may also be members of one or more of the regional economic commissions of the United Nations.

Non-Member States are full members of:

> The Commission on Narcotic Drugs
> The Executive Committee of the High Commissioner's Programme (for Refugees)
> The UN/FAO inter-governmental committee of the World Food Programme
> The Governing Council of the United Nations Development Programme
> The International Development Board of UNIDO
> The Executive Board of UNICEF
> ECE (Economic Commission for Europe)
> ECAFE (Economic Commission for Asia and the Far East)
> UNCTAD
> UNIDO

Of the Non-Member States, the following have a population of less than one million:

> Holy See (Executive Committee of the High Commissioner's Programme for Refugees, UNCTAD and UNIDO)
> Liechtenstein (UNCTAD and UNIDO)
> Monaco (UNCTAD and UNIDO)
> San Marino (UNCTAD and UNIDO)
> Western Samoa (ECAFE and UNIDO)

---

[86] However, many U.N. resolutions provide for the circulation of comments and observations by members of the specialised agencies, who are not members of the United Nations.

Associate membership (without right to vote) exists in ECAFE, ECLA (Economic Commission for Latin America) and ECA (Economic Commission for Africa). Small associate members include:

Brunei (ECAFE)
Hong Kong (ECAFE)
British Honduras [Belize] (ECLA)

The terms of reference of ECA provide that non-self-governing territories in Africa (including islands) are associate members.

Fiji was proposed (in April 1968) as an associate member of ECAFE.

The West Indies Associated States were proposed as a single associate member of ECLA in 1968.

States members of any specialized agency may benefit from United Nations Development Programme activities, even if they are not Members of the United Nations.

IV. SPECIALIZED AGENCIES

The following Members of the United Nations with a population of one million or less are also members of one or more of the specialized agencies:

	IAEA	IIO	FAO	UN-ESCO	WHO	BANK	IFC	IDA	FUND	ICAO	UPU	ITU	WMO	IMCO	GATT
Barbados		X	X	X	X					X	X	X	X		X
Botswana		X	X	X		X		X	X		X	X	X		X [a]
Congo (Brazzaville)		X	X	X	X	X		X	X	X	X	X	X		X
Cyprus	X	X	X	X	X	X		X	X	X	X	X	X		X
Gabon	X	X	X	X	X	X	X	X	X	X	X	X			X
The Gambia			X			X		X	X	X	X	X	X		X [b]
Guyana		X	X	X	X	X	X	X	X	X	X	X	X		X [a]
Iceland	X	X	X	X	X	X	X	X	X	X	X	X	X	X	
Kuwait	X	X	X	X	X	X	X	X	X	X	X	X	X	X	X [b]
Lesotho		X	X	X	X	X	X	X	X	X	X	X			
Luxembourg	X						X	X	X	X	X	X	X		X [b]
Maldive Islands					X						X	X		X	
Malta		X	X	X	X	X	X	X	X	X	X	X	X	X	X
Mauritius		X	X	X	X	X		X	X	X	X	X	X	X	
Trinidad and Tobago	X	X	X	X	X	X	X	X	X	X	X	X	X	X	X

The following States with a population under one million who are not Members of the United Nations are members of one or more of the specialized agencies:

	IAEA	IIO	FAO	UN-ESCO	WHO	BANK	IFC	IDA	FUND	ICAO	UPU	ITU	WMO	IMCO	GATT
Holy See	X										X	X			
Liechtenstein	X										X	X			
Monaco	X			X	X						X	X			
San Marino											X				
Western Samoa					X										

[a] Applying GATT de facto, pending final decision as to their final commercial policy.
[b] Acceded provisionally.

The *135 members* of UPU include the following small territories not listed in the table: Netherlands Antilles and Surinam; Portuguese Provinces in West Africa; Portuguese Provinces in Asia and Oceania; Spanish Territories in Africa; Overseas Territories for whose international relations the Government of the United Kingdom is responsible; whole of the Territories represented by the French Office of Overseas Posts and Telecommunications; whole of the Territories of the United States, including the Trust Territory of the Pacific Islands.

The *133 members* of ITU include the following small territories not listed in the table: Group of Territories represented by the French Overseas Posts and Telecommunication Agency; Overseas Territories for whose international relations the Government of the United Kingdom is responsible; Portuguese Overseas Provinces; Spanish Provinces in Africa; Territories of the United States.

The *132 members* of WMO include 120 states and 12 territories, all of whom maintain their own meteorological services. Besides those small territories listed in the Table, the small members are: British Caribbean Territories; French Polynesia; French Territory of the Afars and Issas; Hong Kong; Netherlands Antilles; New Caledonia; Portuguese West Africa (Equatorial Guinea); Surinam.

The following small states or territories are associate members of one or more specialized agencies:

> Bahrein (FAO, UNESCO, WHO)
> Qatar (FAO, UNESCO, WHO)
> British Eastern Caribbean Group (UNESCO)
> Hong Kong (IMCO)

A survey of provisions of the specialized agencies and the IAEA concerning admission to membership of the specialized agencies indicates[87] that membership in ILO, WHO, UNESCO, ICAO, IMCO, IAEA is restricted to *"States"*; IBRD, IMF, IDA, IFC are limited to *"countries"*; FAO refers to *"nations"*; whereas UPU, ITU and WMO employ more flexible and comprehensive terms:

> UPU refers to any sovereign country; a list of entities considered to be a single member country of the Union or a single postal administration of a member country within the meaning of the UPU Convention.
>
> ITU refers to any country or group of territories listed in Annex I; any country not listed in Annex I which becomes a Member of the United Nations and accedes to the ITU Convention; and any sovereign country, not listed in Annex I and not a Member of the United Nations, which applies for membership in the Union and

[87] Unpublished study made by the Legal Office of the United Nations in November 1967.

receives the approval of two thirds of the members of the Union.
WMO refers to States, and to any territory or group of territories
maintaining its own meteorological services.

*   *   *   *

In the case of *WHO*, when the application of Monaco for full
membership was considered, it was accepted without objection.[88] It is
interesting to note, however, that when the Legal Committee considered
the matter a few days earlier,[89] the representative of Egypt emphasized
the necessity of regarding Monaco's application as an individual case. He
felt that because of its size, Monaco would be unable to contribute to the
finances and activities of the Organization, and that by opening the door
to admitting such small States, there was a danger of overloading the
Organization and weakening its effectiveness.

It was therefore agreed that the admission of Monaco "should
constitute a decision only for this particular case and should not serve as
a precedent for the future."[90]

The application of San Marino was considered in 1949. The
instructions of the observer of San Marino were to "endeavour to obtain
the admission of the Republic of San Marino as an ordinary member of
the WHO on condition however that the annual contribution should be
within its means."[91]

He dwelt upon this matter as follows in a memorandum submitted to
WHO:

> Your Secretariat has informed us that the Republic of San
> Marino should pay an annual contribution of $2,500 or 10,000
> Swiss francs, in order to have the honour of becoming an ordinary
> member of your institution. Unfortunately the country I represent
> cannot assume so heavy a burden. The Republic of San Marino is
> an entirely independent sovereign State with an area of 60 square
> kilometres and a population of 19,000, of which 12,000 live at
> home and 7,000 abroad. 80% are engaged in agriculture. San
> Marino has, therefore, a sort of self-supporting economy. She
> could not exist otherwise, for there are no taxes and her industry is
> in its infancy. Her principal source of revenue consists in the sale
> of stamps, telegrams and so on, together with the customs duties
> paid by the Italian Government. . . . With the best will in the
> world, this small state could not pay such a large annual contribu-
> tion.
> Furthermore the following point which concerns all the

[88] WHO Official Records, First Assembly, p. 76, 10th plenary meeting,
2 July 1948.

[89] *Ibid.*, p. 276, Legal Committee, Second meeting, 30 June 1948.

[90] *Ibid.*, p. 332.

[91] WHO Official Records, Second Assembly, 1949, document A2/CM/
4, p. 6.

so-called small states deserves consideration: The lofty aims incorporated in the statutes and the programme of the WHO are universal and can only be achieved if every single state in the world belongs to the organization and helps in the common task. I should like to raise one point in this connection. One of your aims is to fight and, implicitly, to *forestall* epidemics. What will the WHO do if it does not accept us as members and if an epidemic breaks out in our country? Even if we are not members, the WHO will be obliged to use every means in its power to put a stop to this epidemic if it does not desire the infection to spread to neighbouring member States. This applies with even greater force to the *prevention* of infectious diseases in men and animals.

In conclusion, the observer of San Marino suggested, *inter alia,* that

1. The Constitution of the WHO shall be amended so as to fix a maximum but not a minimum limit to annual contributions.

2. The conception of a small State shall be circumscribed and defined.

3. Special rules shall be drawn up for the admission of new member States under which contributions shall be assessed according to the area of the territory, the population, the economic and financial position and the solvency of the respective States.

The World Health Assembly decided that because the Republic of San Marino had announced it could not withdraw its reservation concerning financial contribution, the Second World Health Assembly could not accept San Marino's application for membership.[92]

Although the matter was not mentioned in the resolution, the Committee on Constitutional Matters had also raised the question of the international status of San Marino in view of its special relationship with Italy.[93]

The WHO Constitution provides that "territories or groups of territories which are not responsible for the conduct of their international relations may be admitted as Associate Members by the Health Assembly if an application is made on behalf of such territory or group of territories by the Member or other authority having responsibility for their international relations."[94]

Detailed provisions regulating the rights and duties of associate members were adopted by the First[95] (1948) and the Second[96] (1949) World Health Assemblies. Associate members may participate without vote in the deliberations of the Health Assembly and its main committees. They may participate with vote and hold office in other committees

[92] WHO Official Record, Second Assembly. resolution WHA 298 and pp. 54, 312 and 355.

[93] WHO Official Records, Second Assembly, p. 312.

[94] FHO Constitution, Article 8.

[95] WHO Official Records, pp. 336-337.

[96] *Ibid.,* document A2/CM/11.

or sub-committees of the Assembly, except the General Committee, the Committee on Credentials and the Nominations Committee. Associate members contribute to the budget of the organization, but difference in status is taken into account in determining their contribution (Qatar and Bahrein, at present associate members, and Mauritius, which was an associate member before independence, pay 0.02 per cent, whereas the minimum assessment for full members is 0.04 per cent). Associate members have all the rights and obligations of full members in the regional organs of the WHO, without the right to vote in the plenary meetings of the regional committees or in sub-divisions dealing with financial or constitutional matters.

Territories not responsible for the conduct of their international relations and not associate members may participate in regional committees. They have the same rights and obligations as associate members, subject to consultation between the States members in the region and the member or other authority having responsibility for the international relations of these territories.

Although the Constitution of WHO contains no provision concerning observers of non-member states, rule 46 of its rules of procedure provides that "observers of invited non-member states and territories on whose behalf application for associate membership has been made may attend any open meetings of the Health Assembly or any of its main committees. They may, upon invitation of the President, and with the consent of the Health Assembly or committees, make a statement on the subject under discussion. Such observers shall have access to non-confidential documents and to such other documents as the Director-General may see fit to make available. They may submit memoranda to the Director-General, who shall determine the nature and scope of their circulation." In 1967, the Holy See and San Marino sent observers to the Twentieth World Health Assembly.

*   *   *   *

ILO has no formal provision in its Constitution for associate membership. Proposals were made for full or associate membership for non-self-governing territories, but were not adopted. However, non-metropolitan territories were invited to send an observer delegation to the ILO Conference. Non-Self-Governing Territories were permitted to attend regional conferences, with a right to vote.

Although the Constitution of ILO contains no provision for observers, Articles 2 and 14 of the Standing Orders of the Conference mention "persons appointed as observers by a State invited to attend a conference." They may, with the permission of the President, address the Conference. In 1965, Barbados, British Guiana and Mauritius sent observers to the ILO Conference.

*   *   *   *

When Monaco applied for membership in *UNESCO* in 1948, its

application was submitted to the Economic and Social Council, in accordance with Article II of the Agreement between the United Nations and UNESCO.[97]

When the matter came up for discussion in the Economic and Social Council, the representative of Canada said, that although he had no doubt of the complete sovereignty of Monaco from the legal point of view, it seemed to him that the Principality did not in fact exercise all the prerogatives of sovereignty because of the treaty binding it to France.[98] He suggested that the Economic and Social Council should decide to offer no objection to the consideration of this application by UNESCO. The draft resolution proposed by Canada contained a last paragraph suggesting "that UNESCO should also consider, in taking its decision, the effect of the precedent which may be set as regards the admission to membership in UNESCO of other diminutive states and of states not fully sovereign."[99] The representative of France did not accept the argument that the admission of Monaco would constitute a precedent for other small states, because the status of Monaco was unique. The last paragraph was modified as follows: "Suggests that the Organization should also consider, in taking its decision, the general problem of the admission of similar diminutive States."[100] When the matter was discussed in the Executive Board,[101] it was recalled that the General Conference had recommended that "each application for membership should be considered on its own merit, taking into consideration particularly the following factors: (a) the legal status of the State in question and its ability to participate in a governmental international organization; (b) the contribution which the State in question is likely to be able to make towards implementing the programme of the Organization it wishes to join."

With regard to the first factor, it was pointed out that the Principality of Monaco was essentially a small, independent state which had bound itself to a more powerful neighbour in some respects, but whose position as a sovereign state had not been prejudiced by the limitations of its freedom of action.

With regard to the second factor, the Executive Board recalled the

[97] Article II of this Agreement provides that for admission of states not Members of the United Nations, the application should be submitted to the Economic and Social Council for recommendation. The Council may recommended the rejection of such application, and such recommendation shall be accepted by the Organization. [This article is not in effect since 1962.]

[98] UNESCO Official Records, Sixth Session, pp. 53-55.

[99] Economic and Social Council Official Records, document E/568/Add.1.

[100] Ibid., resolution 137 (VI), 5 February 1948.

[101] UNESCO 8 EX/6.

considerable activities of the Principality of Monaco in the field of oceanography and its contributions to the theatre and music.

As regards the possible effect of Monaco's admission on the future admission of other diminutive states, the Economic and Social Council pointed out that it was referring to the Republic of San Marino, the Republic of Andorra and Liechtenstein. The position of Monaco was quite a special one, it said, and could not be compared to that of these other states.

As a result of these considerations, the General Conference of UNESCO admitted Monaco, adding that "this decision shall in no way be invoked as a precedent in the event of an application for admission to membership by any other diminutive State."[102]

The original Constitution of UNESCO made no provision for associate membership. In 1948, when the application for (full) membership of Monaco was discussed in the Executive Board, the representative of the United States of America suggested that the Constitution be amended to provide for the admission of similar diminutive states as associate members, and that the application of Monaco be held over until the General Conference had given a decision on such an amendment. This proposal was not accepted, Monaco was admitted and the "complications which would arise from the establishment of the status of associate membership for a Sovereign State" were underlined.[103]

In 1951, the Constitution of UNESCO was amended in order to admit associate members to the Organization. Article II (3) prescribes that "Territories or groups of territories which are not responsible for the conduct of their international relations may be admitted as associate members by the General Conference by a two-thirds majority of members present and voting, upon application made on behalf of such territory or group of territories by the member or other authority having responsibility for their international relations; the nature and extent of the rights and obligations of associate members shall be determined by the General Conference." A resolution adopted at the same time formulates these rights and duties: Associate members have the right to participate without vote in the deliberations of the General Conference and its commissions and committees and other subsidiary organs of the General Conference and the Executive Board. They are not eligible for membership on the Executive Board. They are subject to the same obligations as members, except that the difference in their status is to be taken into account in determining their contribution to the budget of the organization.

[102] UNESCO Official Records, pp. 156-157, Third Session, 15th meeting, 9 December 1948.
[103] UNESCO Executive Board, 8 EX/SR.8 (rev.), 27 September 1948.

The associate members of UNESCO are Bahrein, Qatar and the British Eastern Caribbean Group. Mauritius was an associate member before becoming independent.

Rule 23 (2) of the rules of procedure of UNESCO provides that "Members of the United Nations which are not members of the Unesco, States which are not members of the United Nations nor of the Unesco . . . shall forward to the Director-General the names of their observers, if possible one week before the date fixed for the opening of the session." Rule 67 provides that "observers of non-member States may make oral or written statements in plenary meetings, and in meetings of committees, commissions and subsidiary bodies, with the consent of the presiding officer."

At the 1964 General Conference of UNESCO, there were observers from two non-member States: the Holy See and Western Samoa.

*   *   *   *

FAO. The question of membership for small or diminutive states has not been discussed, and no mini-state has applied for membership.

The Constitution of FAO made no provision for associate membership. But an amendment was adopted in 1955 providing for any territory or group of territories which is not responsible for the conduct of its international relations to become an associate member.

Associate members may participate in the Conference of FAO and its commissions and committees without the right to vote. Associate members contribute to the budget of the organization, and their "contributions are as far as feasible calculated on the same basis as contributions from member nations, the amount thus obtained being reduced by four-tenths to take account of the difference of status between member nations and associate members."[104]

At present only Bahrein and Qatar are associate members of FAO. A number of previously dependent territories were associate members of FAO before becoming independent, at which time they became Members of the United Nations and full members of FAO.

Article XXV (11) of the General Rules provides that "the Council may make arrangements for participation by observers from non-member nations in discussions on particular items of the Council Agenda, in appropriate meetings of the Council or its committees, and for the submission of memoranda."

The Holy See attended the FAO Conference as an observer in 1957 and 1959.

V. OTHER INTERNATIONAL AND REGIONAL ORGANIZATIONS

The problem of smallness does not appear to have affected participation in several international and regional organizations.

---

[104] FAO Financial regulation Rule 5(1).

The *Commonwealth*: Among its twenty-eight members, ten have a population of one million or less: Cyprus, Trinidad and Tobago, Malta, The Gambia, Guyana, Botswana, Lesotho, Barbados, Mauritius, Swaziland. [105, 106] The Commonwealth includes, as parts of larger units, former small territories such as Sabah and Sarawak (as parts of Malaysia) and Zanzibar (as part of Tanzania). In addition, some forty dependencies of Commonwealth countries are included in the Commonwealth, and most of them (with the exception of Hong Kong and the Trust Territory of New Guinea) have populations under 1,000,000.

NATO: Among its fifteen members, two have populations of less than one million: Iceland and Luxembourg.

EEC: Among its six members, only one has population of less than one million: Luxembourg. Among the associated members, two are in this category: Congo (Brazzaville) and Gabon.

OECD: Among its twenty-one members, two have a population under one million: Iceland and Luxembourg.

OAS: Among its twenty-three members, two have populations of one million or less: Barbados and Trinidad and Tobago.

OAU: Among its forty-one members, eight have populations under one million: Congo (Brazzaville), Gabon, The Gambia, Lesotho, Botswana, Swaziland, Mauritius and Equatorial Guinea.

League of Arab States: Among its fourteen members, only one is under the one-million population mark: Kuwait.

South Pacific Commission: Among its six members, two have population under one million: Western Samoa, and Nauru.

VI. OPTIONS WITH REGARD TO PARTICIPATION IN UNITED NATIONS AFFAIRS

The present options or combination of options for small states and territories can be summarized as follows:

(a) *For independent mini-states:*

    (i) full membership in the United Nations;
    (ii) full membership in regional economic commissions, UNCTAD and UNIDO, without United Nations membership;
    (iii) party to the Statute of the International Court of Justice;
    (iv) observer status;

[105] In November 1968, Nauru became a special member of the British Commonwealth. Under the terms of the agreement, Nauru may not be represented at meetings of the Commonwealth Heads of Government. But it will be permitted to participate at ministerial and other official levels in such fields as education, medical co-operation and finance. Moreover, the island is eligible for Commonwealth technical aid.

[106] Tonga, Western Samoa and Fiji have since joined the Commonwealth, bringing the membership to 31.

(v) membership of one or more of the specialized agencies without membership in the United Nations; participation in UNDP activities and invitation to various conferences under United Nations auspices;

(vi) non-membership in the United Nations.

(b) *For dependent mini-territories*:

(i) associated membership in economic commissions;

(ii) participation in delegation of metropolitan country;

(iii) associated membership in one or more specialized agencies;

(iv) appearances through petitioners in United Nations organs.

Among possible options not presently available but conceivable in the future for mini-states and mini-territories, one might mention:

(i) United Nations associated membership (membership with restriction on the right to vote);

(ii) United Nations membership within a system of weighted voting;

(iii) joint membership with other Member State(s);

(iv) limited participation in United Nations affairs;

(v) United Nations special services.

D. PROBLEMS OF DEFENCE AND SECURITY

Defence and national security pose special problems for small states and territories, though the question is of universal concern and importance. For comparatively tiny territories which have neither the manpower nor the resources to create and maintain a defence system adequate for even token resistance, physical and psychological arrangements are essential for security. At one stage of history, small states tried to remain neutral and non-communicative, hoping that they would be ignored by bigger states. But the experience of two world wars in this century alone has shown this approach to be unworkable. Since World War II, small states and territories have had to look for other arrangements.

The historical factors which have influenced the emergence of new states into independence also determine to some extent the direction and form of possible security arrangements for these states. The organs of the United Nations responsible for the maintenance of international peace and security, together with other appropriate bodies, have tried to make arrangements under which the sovereignty and territorial integrity of some of the territories can be preserved and, if possible, guaranteed by the United Nations. Discussion in the United Nations was devoted to devising special machinery to supplement the collective security arrangements envisaged under the Charter. While strict adherence to the principles of the Charter by all Member States would obviate any need for special arrangements, the United Nations Members have recognized the possibility of non-observance of these principles by some Member States and consequently the need for further safeguards.

In particular, the case of certain territories in Southern Africa have been of grave concern to the United Nations. It was in regard to the former High Commission Territories in Southern Africa, Botswana, Lesotho and Swaziland, that the United Nations was faced with the question of providing an adequate guarantee from external aggression to these states. It was a matter of continuing concern to the United Nations that these territories had been claimed by the "minority racialist" Government in the Republic of South Africa. Successive resolutions adopted by the General Assembly before these territories became independent included no concrete steps, but the operative paragraph of General Assembly resolution 1954 (XVIII) of 11 December 1963 stated that "the General Assembly solemnly warns the Government of the Republic of South Africa that any attempt to annex or encroach upon the territorial integrity of these three Territories shall be considered an act of aggression."

In regard to South-West Africa (Namibia), the General Assembly[107] called upon South Africa to remove all bases and other military installations located in the territory and to refrain from utilizing the territory in any way whatsoever as a military base for internal or external purposes. It also declared that the continued foreign occupation by South Africa of the Territory of South-West Africa constituted a grave threat to international peace and security. But South Africa has continued to refuse to comply with the United Nations demands that it withdraw from the former mandated territory.

Military bases are another aspect of defence that bears discussion. The United Nations has taken no action on the question of military bases in independent states, though recognizing its relevance. However, in regard to military bases in territories which are not yet independent, the United Nations, particularly the Committee of Twenty-Four, has devoted much time and effort.

It has examined the situation in the Pacific (Guam, the Trust Territory of the Pacific Islands, Papua-New Guinea), in the Caribbean (Bermuda, United States Virgin Islands, Bahamas), in the Indian Ocean (British Indian Ocean Territory) and in the Mediterranean (Gibraltar), and has concluded[108] that "strategic military considerations are an important factor in prolonging colonial rule in many parts of the world" and that "on the whole, military activities and arrangements by colonial powers in territories under their administration constitute a serious impediment to the implementation of the Declaration on the Granting of Independence to Colonial Countries and Peoples."

The administering Powers, i.e., the United Kingdom, the United

---

[107] General Assembly resolution 2372 (XXII) of 12 June 1968, and previous resolutions.
[108] A/7200 (Part II), p. 38.

States of America and Australia, have expressed their complete disagreement with these views, stating that in the majority of dependent territories with which the Committee was concerned, there was no military or defence presence whatsoever. In the small number of territories with a military presence, they claimed, it was necessary to maintain these territories against a possible external threat. Further, they asserted, such military presence in no way impeded decolonization.

Many of the military bases were discontinued by the authorities. Others have been continued by agreement, partly for reasons of military security and partly because in some small territories the bases provide the main source of foreign income and large-scale employment.

While it is contended that the existence of military bases in small territories would adversely affect their march to independence, it is also said that the existence of military bases after independence often serves to bolster security. It must be recognized, however, that in the event of military confrontation between opposing powers, the small states with military bases might be more vulnerable to outside attack. This situation is intimately connected with the question of military alliances and regional defence arrangements.

Outside of universal arrangements available through the United Nations, small states have also sought security through regional and other group alignments. From the experience of such regional arrangements (also envisaged under Chapter VIII of the Charter of the United Nations) over two decades, it is evident that they are of limited usefulness. These arrangements also have disadvantages which affect the junior partners. But it has to be borne in mind that small states enter into these arrangements in their own national interest.

The question is whether this is a pattern which can be adopted by other small states in furthering their national interest. Analyzing existing arrangements and their effectiveness in preventing outside interference, one can only conclude that, like the collective security system envisaged under the United Nations Charter, regional arrangements are not sufficient for the needs of small states.

Many observers feel that bilateral or small group arrangements have worked out better than the universal and regional or bloc arrangements. Many small states which gained independence in the post-World War II period have found it useful to continue defence association with the former colonial Power. The disadvantages arising from bilateral arrangements should also be taken into account, however. These range from the direct and indirect influence which the bigger partners can exert on the small states to the possibility of being dragged into unnecessary wars by mutual defence pacts. Complete identity of interests and views is almost impossible under any circumstances.

There is much to be said for the pragmatic view that small states should not rely on any one specific method, but resort to different types of security arrangements. There is a strong element of insurance in such a course of action. A balanced combination of principal reliance on one single country or small group of countries, participation in regional arrangements and membership in the United Nations would seem to give the utmost security for defense and the necessary flexibility for conduct of foreign relations. Even this arrangement is not a water-tight guarantee, but then there is no such thing.

The internal aspects of security fall primarily within the domestic jurisdiction of the state. Nevertheless, some of these problems spill over into the international arena. Internal security is not always an exclusive concern of a particular government. Thus when the troops in a particular country rebelled against the existing legitimate government, it was necessary to seek the intervention of the troops of the former colonial Power. There have been many such incidents where internal revolts were quelled with the help of foreign troops. This raises the question of the optimum strength of troops to be maintained by a small state, and the question of security in these cases.

Even though there are no definite solutions to the national security problems of small states and territories, it may be useful to propose certain practical approaches which small states might adopt. One approach is the creation of cooperative arrangements with neighbouring countries, not excluding former administering Powers, as with the Cook Islands and New Zealand. A second approach is for the small states themselves to appreciate some of the limitations on resources and capabilities inherent in their situation, and to fashion their foreign and domestic policies accordingly.

Finally, they should collectively make more energetic efforts to evolve new systems of collective security arrangements under the auspices of the United Nations, consonant with changing patterns of international relationships. Neutralization and recognition of the status of non-alignment are elements of a new system which requires radical changes in attitudes towards bloc politics. This approach is already apparent in some circles. Since no general criteria or guidelines can be evolved for small states and territories as a whole, practical procedures in regard to military strength, logistics and resources can only be considered for each small state and territory individually. That is beyond the scope of the present study, however.

CHAPTER THREE

PUBLIC ADMINISTRATION PROBLEMS[1]

Small states have both advantages and disadvantages from an administrative standpoint. Smallness can facilitate administrative co-ordination and integration and promote responsiveness of officials and employees to the public will. There are presumably other administrative advantages. Substantial evidence shows, however, that small states face unusual difficulties in planning, financing, staffing and operating their administrative services, because of the relatively small scale on which activities must be carried out.

An effort was made to distinguish between administrative problems associated with underdevelopment and those associated with smallness. Many small countries are underdeveloped, and as such face numerous administrative difficulties similar to those faced by larger states in comparable stages of development. This preliminary report identified those administrative problems likely to arise from smallness and others which, although universal, appear to be more troublesome in smaller countries.

Whether in large states or small, public administration operates within a complex political, social, geographical and economic environment, and cannot be dissociated from that environment. However, these variables are mentioned only as they have a direct and appreciable effect on the internal administration of small states.

Small states have certain common characteristics that bear upon their administrative systems. The material resources of these states are often limited. If one is small in area, the range of crops or mineral products may be restricted. If it is large in area, it may need sizeable investments in infrastructure to develop its resources. The small state may have to concentrate on development of a few products or a single product on which its revenue may largely depend, adjusting its plans to their yield and their vulnerability to natural disasters or fluctuations of world markets.

A small state is usually limited in its personnel resources, which affects administration in two ways: the national manpower pool on which the state can draw to staff its public services is limited in size, and the skill of available personnel may be restricted by limited education and training facilities. At the same time, the small state may need to take into account that only a few persons will need a particular service. It will have to consider whether it has the financial and personnel resources to provide service for so few persons, and whether the service itself is technically feasible if its clientele is below a minimum number. Examples include an internal airline, a cancer treatment unit or a university graduate school. Similar questions arise with regard to provision of many other public

---

[1] This Chapter has been contributed by the Public Administration Division, Department of Economic and Social Affairs of the United Nations Secretariat. In preparing this Chapter, the Division has called upon United Nations Public Administration experts who have worked in small states for their views and suggestions.

services, such as intensive treatment of rare diseases, public transport to remote areas, specialized libraries or education in advanced subjects.

Social factors are likely to have an especially acute effect on administration in small states. Most notable is the unusually strong influence of family and personal relations on decision-making and on civil service recruitment and career advancement in many of the small countries. In states whose area as well as population is small, public reaction to government measures may be mobilized quickly and thus rapidly affect government activity. Where the population is divided into conflicting communal groups, their conflicts may have an especially strong and rapid impact on government. Conversely, in a small state with an extensive area, persons or groups far from administrative centres sometimes find it difficult to make their desires felt or to secure their share of services.

Many small states are island states, or are in other ways geographically or culturally remote from neighbours. In fact, this isolation often is a major reason for their separate constitutional existence and the difficulties in obtaining common services. It can have an inhibiting effect on the development of regional (supra-national) institutions or on efforts to operate public services, especially if active nationalism is involved. It also may produce a professional/technical isolation which restricts the interchange of information.

One expert pointed out that in the administration of small states there is sometimes "another central factor of vital importance, even more than whether a state may be rich or poor, large or small. This is whether any sudden change has occurred in the economic or social structure of the state, moving it from one level of administrative requirements to a totally different one. For example, acute problems may arise from the break-up of a federal structure with the creation of new small national units, or the sudden accretion of wealth to an impoverished area." Recent changes of this nature have been felt by a number of small countries, while the majority of small states are still affected by the complex changes required to adjust their administration to independent conditions.

Another major problem that exists in all developing countries but is especially acute in small states is that administrative capability must be taken into account in setting development targets or goals in terms of quality of public services. Small states may have the problem of increasing that capability through co-operative arrangements with other countries or restricting their goals to the extent of growth in their own administrative capability.

In addition to differences among small states in population, area and density, there are differences in wealth, isolation and cultural homogeneity. The impact of these differences on administration is unique to each state and requires individual treatment. Yet the observations of experts who have worked in small countries, and the evidence from a multitude of reports on the administration of such countries, point to a number of administrative problems which appear common to many small countries and seem to be caused or intensified by their small size. These problems will be considered in more detail.

A. ORGANIZATION

Upon achieving independence, a small state becomes subject to pressures to establish a wide range of services and an organizational structure common to larger countries. Much of this pressure may be necessary, but it may also be beyond the resources of the country. A large number of ministries are frequently set up.[2] In addition, as one expert commented, a "tendency to establish within ministries an excessive number of tiny administrative units each devoted to a narrow specialized range of work inevitably results in an equally excessive number of hierarchial layers of administration. Both lead to excessive staffing, excessive desk-to-desk movement of work, and slack articulation of the steps in administrative processes."

Not all of the difficulty arises from the large number of administrative units. Equally important is the problem of grouping, relating and structuring activities so that administrative units are fitted to the specific needs and resources of the small country. Most countries have inherited an organization adapted to colonial status or to internal self-government rather than to full independence, and this organization has usually drawn heavily on the practices of other colonies or of the former metropolitan Power. In the early years of independence, the new country has the problem of revising the structure to meet its individual needs.

Several experts have recommended that small states should endeavour to:

(a) Keep the number of individual ministries small by grouping related activities under the supervision of a single minister. It was pointed out that in a small country only a few activities, such as finance, are sizeable enough to warrant an individual ministry. Others, for which there are separate ministries in large countries, may have to be combined under fewer ministers in order to minimize overhead and best utilize personnel. The minimization of the number of ministries may result in denying ministerial rank to a number of leaders of a governing party or factions thereof and may be strenuously opposed for partisan reasons. This problem, also common in larger countries, is especially difficult in small countries, where it may lead to a multiplicity of very small ministries and to a great variation in their size and consequent work load.

[2] *The United Nations Handbook of Public Administration* (p. 19) defines a ministry as "A grouping of government functions or departments headed by a major political officer known as a minister. In some countries such a grouping is called a department and is headed by a secretary." In the present document, the term "ministry" will include both types.

(b) Use each department or section within a ministry to cover the widest practicable range of services, and avoid fragmenting them into highly specialized units. This will conserve administrative manpower as well as facilitate co-ordination in programme operation. It will also reduce the chance of creating numerous specialized posts for which specialists are not available. Obviously, consolidation should not reach the point where it curtails the provision of needed services.

(c) Simplify procedures to promote optimum use of available manpower and skills, and to take advantage of the face-to-face contact made more feasible by small-scale operations.

(d) Integrate or at least co-ordinate central and local government organization and staffing to the fullest extent possible.

B. LEADERSHIP AND DECISION-MAKING

Many of the factors affecting administrative decisions are common to states regardless of size. However, one public administration expert carefully summarized those which, in his experience, seem to have a substantially greater impact in small states. He states them as follows:

(a) The rôle of the individual—his assumed rights, his responsibilities, his political sensitivity and the vocal expression of his personal and national ambitions—takes on greater significance.

(b) The individual, as a member of a group, is more susceptible to pressures, both internal and external, and will react more spontaneously to them, generally in ways which may more readily be predicted.

(c) Pressure groups will be smaller, though not necessarily less vocal, and their objectives will tend to be more short-term.

(d) Criticism becomes more personal.

(e) Politicians exercise greater influence, frequently based more on personal than on party factors;

(f) Senior administrative and political office holders have more direct contact with the man in the street, and there is less of the aloofness traditionally associated with a bureaucracy.

(g) Decision-making becomes more closely associated with personal risk and promotes a search for acceptable substitutes.

Perhaps the primary features of leadership and decision-making in small states are the intimate nature of the exercise of power and the intensely personal character of reactions to that exercise. Evidence from social studies and from the experience of experts emphasizes the especially heavy pressure of personal commitments in a small and close-knit society. Pressure from family, friends and politicians will be brought to bear on ministers, senior administrators, and in fact on all civil servants, far more so than in larger countries, where the decision-making process is more systematized and impersonal.

Senior administrators in a small country often find it difficult to secure reliable data. While they are usually personally familiar with local conditions, they are not able to secure all the unbiased technical, financial, statistical and similar information which in larger countries is collected and published by or received from external sources. Often such information is not available within the country; relevant comparative data from outside is hard to secure; junior staff to collect data is less numerous than in large countries; and extra-departmental resources such as universities, libraries, commercial associations, etc., are not adequately endowed for the purpose.

Even when decisions have been made, the social pressures in a small state to negate them are so intense that the state may be unable either to resist the pressures or to develop suitable machinery to implement the decisions.

One expert felt that the special impact of personal relationships in a small state is reflected not so much in actual misfeasance or malfeasance by officials as in their reluctance to carry through vigorously any official act which might offend some person or group. He pointed out that there is no easy means of resolving this problem, aside from improved training for public servants and education of the public to support impartiality in the discharge of official duties.

On the other hand, it was suggested that this community closeness in small states, while often creating difficulties, can also produce positive benefits for administration. Government touches the citizen directly; it is not a far-off mystery. The acts of government on everyday matters are often the subject of daily conversation, and the problem of communication between government and citizens is greatly reduced. It thus may be easier to enlist the community's assistance in making public action more effective.

C. COMMUNICATION AND CO-ORDINATION

There is some evidence that heavy reliance in small states on informal means of communication tends to inhibit the flow and retention of information in administration. Gaps or blockages frequently occur, either by chance or through personal frictions or group jealousies. The situation is made worse by insufficient recording of decisions and actions.

A small country often lacks the machinery for formal co-ordination, yet, any tightening of its administrative structure demands extra efforts in co-ordination. It has been suggested that ministers each charged with various responsibilities yet lacking large personal staffs will need to rely greatly on a small but highly effective cabinet secretariat to co-ordinate all matters of inter-ministerial concern. This may be separate from, or combined with, a vigorous Office of the Prime Minister, since in a small country's organization the Prime Minister almost inevitably must carry an especially heavy burden of co-ordination. It should be noted that in a small country, the Prime Minister is likely also to act as Minister of

Foreign Affairs or of Defence. Thus he will need an office to help co-ordinate his own varied responsibilities as well as to assist in his over-all co-ordinative rôle.

Within each ministry, especially if the minister is responsible for varied functions, improved internal co-ordination is essential. The minister will again need able personal help to keep track of his varied responsibilities; he will need to allocate substantial time for direct consultation with each of his senior administrative subordinates. He may need to preside in person over periodic group sessions.

D. CIVIL SERVICE

Recruitment of appropriate staff is especially difficult in small states because of the limited opportunities in these states for preliminary training or experience, especially in management and in specialized and technical subjects. Senior posts are few, promotions consequently rare and opportunities to rise in specialization infrequent. Retaining the most highly qualified in the public service is usually precarious, because the government cannot offer careers with substantial prospects of advancement.

Small countries themselves should provide a substantial amount of in-service training for their civil servants. Many now rely heavily on training in other countries, which is usually costly and requires the extended absence of the trainee. Also, few persons are qualified to fill the officials jobs while they are undergoing training. Several analysts have commented that trainees from small countries who are sent overseas are especially likely upon return to be lost permanently to other organizations.

A special disadvantage of foreign training is the difference in scale and specialization, as well as in technical level, between the small country and the country of training. Consequently, the trainee from a small country may find difficulty in properly adapting the training experience to his job at home.

In view of all this, joint or multi-national schemes for training the personnel of two or more small states are frequently proposed. Such arrangements are most feasible where the states are neighbours and have similar working languages, administrative structures and procedures. Programmes can include not only formal institutes and courses, but more informal arrangements, and they need not always be centred in one country. Some types of co-operative training are possible, with each participating state specializing in training for the entire region in certain subjects.

Thus it appears that most civil service training in small states must be done at home. This includes virtually all training of subordinate staff and most training of specialists and managers.

Another problem, however, is the difficulty in securing qualified trainers. A small country will be especially dependent on a local university or other community resources to supplement its training staff. In addition, departmental training may have to rely heavily on part-time use of officials who already have the necessary knowledge and who know how to teach it.

The use of foreign experts as trainers is often less practicable in small countries than in larger ones. Few small countries can carry the costs of the unusually large range of trainers needed, even if many are provided through technical assistance programmes. Often the number of personnel to be trained will not warrant the long-term employment of a specialized trainer, although he may be able to divide his time among several countries. Frequently, foreign trainers are specialists who lack the broad experience needed for a training programme in a small country.

Development of local resources for training and research, for instance through a university, has the special value of producing permanent facilities, whereas outside help is often merely temporary. Even if the local training and research is initially less proficient than that which outsiders might provide, it may be better adjusted to local background and needs, and it frequently has a greater continuing influence on local policies.

It would appear that a multiple approach is required, including some use of outside experts with broad abilities, as much multi-national training and interchange with neighbours as possible, fullest use of all available local resources and strong emphasis on outside help to "train the trainers," who will then be available locally on a continuing basis.

Many of the social and personal pressures which affect all administration in a small state will be felt most strongly in its personnel administration. At every point of recruitment, promotion, reassignment, disciplining and even retirement, individual or group loyalties may compete with the general good of the service.

As was pointed out by one expert, personal factors in a small country also tend to have an undue effect on any system of personnel rating and reporting. Senior officials become especially reluctant to make any adverse reports on staff because of the immediacy and intimacy of personal, political or even trade union reactions. The advancement of the meritorious employee tends to be on a par with the mediocre one. In the absence of an effective merit system, seniority remains the dominant factor in staff promotions. This makes for an unfortunate influence on morale in a small civil service.

One analyst has suggested that a small country might consider employing a professional "national manager" from another state. The more limited area of personnel management is possibly the best place for such outside professional objectivity to be tested.

Reference has been made constantly to the career limitations produced by the small scale of administration in these states. Those limitations can be eased if the public service is made as broad and unified as possible. A small state may find it desirable to combine its national civil service with those of local government, public corporations and public educational and research institutions, for instance. In this way, individuals could hope for wider careers through transfer and promotion, while the state could profit from the economies of larger-scale personnel administration.

Many suggestions have been made for combatting the scarcity of technical staff to carry out national development projects in small countries. One is to encourage exchange of staff with non-governmental organizations. Another is to use the military to supplement inadequate civilian administrative resources; in this way, development and technical work such as communications can be co-ordinated with maintenance and training of the armed forces. A number of small states have thus been able to improve and expand work in such fields as rural development, public works, air transport, radio communications and protection of coastal fisheries and commerce.

Unless the personnel system as a whole is effective, efforts to improve recruitment and training have little meaning. This is true of all states, but certain special needs of small states may be noted. If officers are asked to perform broader rather than specialized jobs, they will need careful job descriptions. If organization units are few and small, the classification of jobs and the opportunities for transfer may require special attention. If community pressures and sensitivity are high, there is all the more reason for systems of supervision and discipline to be clear, fair, and firmly established. If the number of higher posts is small, officers will be especially concerned with matters of promotions, career advancement, pay increments and pensions. None of these problems are unique to small countries; taken together, however, they do indicate that a well balanced, efficient, comprehensive personnel system is the key to effective administration.

E. LOCAL GOVERNMENT

As earlier suggested, a small state must adapt its administrative structure to its special circumstances. This is especially applicable in designing levels of government and relationships between levels. In a state that is small in area as well as population, it may be possible to achieve a large degree of consolidation of central and local government, with the national administration performing many or all functions that elsewhere would be performed by local authorities. Even if separate local governing bodies exist, ways may be devised so that the actual administration of most technical services is part of a national system. In contrast, a small state with an extensive territory may find that difficulties of communication and sparsity of population make it inadvisable for the national government to administer some services directly. In such a situation, it may prove best to devolve substantial authority to local government units and provide necessary technical assistance to them.

Even states whose territory is small may find intangible advantages in maintaining some system of local government. One expert argued that in a small country, the central departments may be

> clogged with a great mass of small individual cases, a large proportion of which could with advantage be siphoned off. Moreover, some of the functions which are often performed by local government, for instance the provision of local amenities, would often be more effectively carried out if some persons more immediately involved were concerned. Again, there would be much civic advantage to be derived from local government as a training ground for national politics and national public office.

Much local administration might be performed by part-time or even volunteer personnel, with consequent savings on salaries.

A small state may have inherited from its colonial past a rather elaborate system of local government which demands a sizeable body of trained manpower and considerable central support and supervision. In the early days of independence, local government may continue to need strong central direction, but the aim should be to devolve as much decision-making as possible to the local level, depending on its resources and the size of units. Central control can continue to be exercised through approval of financial estimates, provision of funds, and, where appropriate, by inspection. Local efforts can be stimulated through grants-in-aid which call for local contribution. However, as noted below, the valuation of real property for tax purposes, the computation of the taxes and, in many cases, their collection, may need to be done by a central expert staff to ensure equity throughout the country.

In any event, a small state will need to take special care to ensure equity throughout its area in matters of financial burden, personnel administration, and quality of services. A recent writer has pointed out that in many small countries, there is really no psychological difference between town and country. Not only does the countryman see the possibilities of public service more directly, but he is able to make his demands felt more directly. However, a number of small states find much of their population concentrated in a few areas, with the resulting danger that services too will be concentrated there. Those who inhabit outlying areas may be neglected, especially since it may be extremely difficult and costly to provide them with services on the scale enjoyed by the majority.

F. PUBLIC FINANCE

While the financial authorities of small countries have no greater responsibility than those of large countries to ensure that public funds are spent wisely, their task is made more difficult by the personal and social pressures already emphasized and by the dearth of experts in budgetary and financial matters.

A special factor of difficulty is what may be called the "diseconomy of size." Some efforts have been made to study the extent to which costs of public services are higher when their scale of operation and number of citizen-clients are smaller. Interestingly, although the evidence is inconclusive, analysts continue to insist that costs *per capita* are higher in small countries than in large ones. In a few small states, this may be attributable to the high degree of urbanization of the population. In any case, since resources of small states are ordinarily very limited, and since administrative operations must be economical, further investigation of the relationship between cost of services and size of population may be desirable. One very fruitful line of approach would be to search for the minimum areas for optimum administration of various specialized services. Some preliminary insights into the question may be seen in the United Nations Public Administration Division's study of Decentralization for National and Local Development,[3] a study in which UNESCO, WHO, FAO and the United Nations Office of Social Affairs in Geneva provided papers on the minimum area for optimal co-ordinated administration of their respective services at the local level. These took into consideration optimum specialist/clientele ratios, need for administrative supervision and cost factors. For example, the WHO paper indicated that a neuro-surgeon could serve a population of one to two million. A similar study of the "minimum area" required for effective administration of high-cost services might help the governments of small states decide whether to provide a service directly or seek co-operative or joint arrangements with other states.

A very few small states are extremely wealthy. They have, however, their own set of problems in public administration. They too find difficulty in staffing administrative offices with able citizens, but they are better able to hire expatriates to satisfy present needs. They recognize the desirability of spending their wealth on wise developmental projects, and increasingly they are noticing the problems of permanent financing and staffing of the operations of capital projects. To a growing extent, they are finding it advisable to use public wealth for projects and services that benefit the general citizenry. Concern is also mounting over social difficulties which may arise when revenues decline and luxury services become too costly to maintain at present levels. Finally, these small states are increasingly concerned about the extent to which their over-staffed public service establishments are manned by non-nationals and about the difficulties of attracting qualified citizens to form a permanent public service.

International experts who have worked in small countries invariably

[3] United Nations Sales No. 62 II.H.2.

emphasize the necessity of establishing in those countries, whether rich or poor, efficient systems for planning and budgeting. They stress that these functions must be manned by qualified personnel. A small country may have unusual difficulties in finding and training such personnel and may initially require special outside assistance in getting qualified officers and setting up the needed systems. The experts emphasize the necessity for courage and "toughness" in the offices of financial administration, although they recognize that social, political and economic pressures in a small state may make such an attitude especially difficult to maintain.

Experts with special experience in taxation in small states emphasize that it is very difficult for such states to secure qualified personnel in the valuation of real property for tax purposes and the computation and collection of taxes. Therefore they strongly recommend, especially in such states, measures to centralize assessment and collection in order to ensure that the burden of taxation is spread as fairly as possible. The revenue needs of local government units, if any, could be met through local taxes, supplemented, if necessary, by grants-in-aid and other revenues, as in larger states.

G. Joint arrangements

In discussions of administration in small states, the proposal is invariably made that somehow those states should seek practicable ways of operating or staffing some of their activities jointly with other states. As earlier noted, there are many practical reasons why joint action is generally difficult. To those can be added the national pride associated with sovereignty, especially in newly independent countries. In view of all these factors and of the great diversity of small states, it is not appropriate here to suggest specific cases where joint action might be explored. Such action should nevertheless be viewed as a useful alternative which may in some cases hold substantial technical and financial advantages for the states concerned. The areas where such arrangements may be fruitful include advanced education and training, interchange of staff for training and professional visits, use of national and foreign specialists and contracting with neighbors for highly technical, costly or unusual services. Many such arrangements already exist. For example, joint universities are found in southern and eastern Africa, and in the latter, an East African Common Services Organisation (EACSO) provides transport and communications services. A common university exists for Botswana, Lesotho and Swaziland. Joint universities also exist in the Caribbean (University of the West Indies) and are contemplated in the Pacific. Under international stimulation, joint regional organizations have been established for such varied services as control of civil aviation traffic, fisheries and desert locusts. Small states contract with others for diplomatic or consular representation in certain countries or cities. The report of the recent Institute of Commonwealth Studies Seminar on the Problems of Smaller Territories notes joint sharing of police, judicial and audit services in the West Indies. An analysis of the existing joint administrative arrangements involving small states would be useful, as it might provide guides for the design of such arrangements in the future and encourage officials of small states to consider additional possibilities for co-operative action.

H. EXTERNAL CONTACT AND INFORMATION

While contact among officials within a small state is very frequent, they often have great difficulty in meeting colleagues from other countries or in learning of relevant administrative developments elsewhere. Many small states are geographically isolated; funds for travel on professional visits and to international meetings are limited; qualified officials cannot be released from work to travel abroad; locally, there are few or limited collections of professional literature; and visitors on official business or tourism are few.

At the same time, the officials of small states usually do not have professional associations, publications and meetings which in larger states provide a basis for professional stimulation and growth. Many officials of small countries live in professional isolation, cut off from contact with others who handle similar problems.

Special efforts are clearly needed to encourage and at times even to finance growth of personal contact and interchange of information. Personal contact might be increased substantially by greater efforts to route official travel of qualified personnel from larger countries through small states, and by outside subsidies for officials of small countries to visit their counterparts in small neighbouring countries. Professional periodicals might well give greater emphasis to recording the problems and actions of small states and ensuring that officials of other states receive that information. Small states can benefit greatly from the fullest possible participation in the meetings and other activities of appropriate regional and international professional associations.

Books on public administration as well as periodicals have very naturally concentrated on the operations of large countries. Little comparative material exists on small states as such. There is need for documentation on administration in smaller countries and analysis of ways in which it can be improved, taking account of the differing circumstances in these countries. Much of that literature may have to be written by officials of the small states themselves or by foreigners who have worked closely with them over substantial periods. Resources are needed to produce this information and make it widely available.

I. TECHNICAL ASSISTANCE

Small states often lack the administrative machinery to plan and utilize large-scale assistance. Counterpart staff are especially hard to recruit, while potential counterparts already with the government may be overloaded with responsibilities. Voluminous assistance may be offered because of the country's small size, weakness and obvious need; however, that assistance may even tend to inhibit the country's own willingness to exert special effort towards national development. In some cases, the country may need help in improving its machinery and its capacity to utilize assistance; the forms and subjects of assistance may need to be adjusted to ensure that the country can make the greatest and most effective use of what is offered.

Thus assistance to a small country in matters of public administration must be planned with careful consideration of the recipient country's over-all capacity to absorb that assistance, and must be concentrated on areas of priority need, with special regard to its multiplier effect. The various experts associated with the United Nations Public Administration Division in this study have suggested several ways in which assistance could be most effective.

It would be uneconomical to provide small states with the wide range of administrative specialists which each might need or desire. At the same time, experience proves it undesirable to assign an expert to visit briefly several small countries at once. Many problems require the steady assistance of outside experts over a considerable time, even though full-time attention may be unnecessary. When short visits by an expert are sufficient, for instance when a well qualified national official can carry on with the periodic help of an expert, then regional or interregional advisers attached to two or more countries (i.e., "multi-national advisers") might be used.

Another possibility would be to assign to small countries experts who are well qualified generally in all aspects of public administration. Such men can assist with a number of administrative needs at once, dividing their time on a priority basis. Where major specialized problems arise which are beyond their competence, short-term specialist experts can be brought in, with the general adviser planning their visits, working with them during their brief stays and following up the results.

Personnel of the OPEX type may be needed where small countries lack qualified persons for certain key posts.[4] In some cases, an OPEX

---

[4] Under the OPEX programme, the United Nations carries out international recruitment of persons for the service of a requesting government to fill operational, executive and administrative posts until local personnel can be trained to take over their duties. During their assignments, they are vested with the same powers, duties and responsibilities as would be a national official of the country itself. The country pays the normal local salary for the post, and that is supplemented by the United Nations up to a level equal to that which the individual would receive as an international advisory expert. Somewhat similar arrangements have been made in certain bilateral assistance programmes.

officer with prestige as well as ability may be especially helpful in the early stages of setting up new administrative systems. An OPEX officer with experience in other small countries would probably be more useful than one with experience in larger countries only.

Mention has been made earlier of assistance which can be provided through information, professional contact and training. Much of this assistance requires use of fellowships, defined rather broadly. In many cases, study visits to other small countries or attendance at regional or international seminars may be more helpful than formal study abroad. In other cases, small countries may consider it more fruitful to send officials on secondment for extensive on-the-job training in similar countries. Special seminars and workshops for officers having common responsibilities in small states should also be organized.

Along with these various forms of technical assistance, additional studies are needed to provide guidelines for improving administration. The subjects meriting priority include the following:

(a) Description and comparative analysis of the existing organization and administration, including personnel systems, of a number of small states.

(b) Either as part of (a) above or separately, a study of existing administrative arrangements for common services among small states or between small and large states.

(c) Studies of optimum minimum units for administration of certain specialized services which governments of small states should consider providing jointly.

PART III: ACTION WHICH THE UNITED NATIONS MIGHT CONSIDER IN FAVOUR OF VERY SMALL STATES AND TERRITORIES

CHAPTER ONE

OPTIONS

A. FOR SMALL DEPENDENT TERRITORIES

I. GENERAL—ROLE OF THE UNITED NATIONS

There seems to be general agreement that small dependent territories have special problems to take into account when the time comes for them to decide on their future status. The idea that there are options to be considered and that unqualified independence is not necessarily the only answer has been recognized not only in a General Assembly resolution,[1] but more recently, with special reference to mini-territories, by the Special Committee of Twenty-Four.[2]

---

[1] General Assembly resolution 1541 (XV) of 15 December 1960. Principle VI: A Non-Self-Governing Territory can be said to have reached a full measure of self-government by
    (a) emergence as a sovereign independent state;
    (b) free association with an independent state; or
    (c) integration with an independent state.

[2] *Inter alia*: *A/6300/Rev.1* (Addendum to agenda item 23, XXI GA), p. 769 on the United States Virgin Islands: "It [the Special Committee] also invites the administering Power to ensure that the people of the Territory are fully aware of the various alternatives open to them, in their achievement of the objectives of General Assembly resolution 1514 (XV)."

    A/6300/Rev.1 (Addendum to agenda item 23, XXI GA), pp. 769 and 770 on the British Islands in the Caribbean: "It [the Special Committee] also expresses its belief that particularly in the case of small Territories, the United Nations should take appropriate steps to ensure that the people of these territories are enabled to express themselves freely on their future status and in full knowledge of the options available to them."

    A/6700/Add.14 (Part II), p. 130, on the United States Virgin Islands: "It [the Special Committee] also invites the administering Power to encourage open, free and public discussion of the various alternatives open to them in their achievement of the objectives of General Assembly resolution 1514 (XV) and to ensure that the people of the Territory shall exercise their right of self-determination in full knowledge of these alternatives."

    A/6700/Add.14 (Part II), p. 131, on the British Virgin Islands: "It [the Special Committee] invites the administering Power to encourage open,

The general practice, however, has been for the administering Power concerned to take exclusive responsibility for outlining the various "options" to the people of the small dependent territory and discussing these options with them, without accepting the participation of outside bodies, such as the United Nations, in this process of enlightenment and discussion."[3]

It has been contended that some form of participation by the United Nations would be beneficial both to the people of the emergent small territory and to the administering Power concerned. It would give the participants a wider outlook by drawing attention to precedents elsewhere and to successful and unsuccessful experiences in similar situations in other parts of the world. The administering Power may not always be fully familiar with those situations, or may not appreciate their relevancy. United Nations participation would encourage fuller discussion. It would add an element of objectivity and relieve a feeling of pressure—justified or unjustified—which the presence of the administering Power as lone partner in discussions may cause. It would help reduce possible doubts about the degree of awareness of other options and of popular acceptance of the formula agreed upon. There would be less controversy in the international forum when the choice of the new status was being ratified by the population concerned and presented to the United Nations as a

---

free and public discussion of the possible options from which the people can make its choice in the efforts to obtain the objectives of General Assembly resolution 1514 (XV) and other resolutions of the General Assembly concerning their Territory, and to ensure that the people of the Territory will be able to exercise its right of self-determination in full knowledge of the options open to it."

A/6700Add.14 (Part II), p. 133, on the six British Associated States in the Caribbean: "It [the Special Committee] requests the administering Power to ensure that the peoples of the Territories are informed of the various possibilities available to them in their achievement of the objectives of resolution 1514 (XV) . . . The Special Committee reiterates its belief that a United Nations presence during the procedures connected with the process of self-determination will be essential in order to ensure that the peoples of the Territories are enabled to exercise their right in complete freedom, without any restriction and in full knowledge of the options available to them."

[3] In one case, however, the United Nations was to some extent involved in the elaboration of the options. In October 1962, the Governments of Senegal and The Gambia (the latter with the consent of the United Kingdom Government) requested the Secretary-General to appoint a team of experts "to lay before the Governments economic and political data on which discussions can be taken as to the form which their future relationships should take." In 1964, a team of four United Nations experts submitted a report "on the alternatives for association between The Gambia and Senegal."

In various other cases, a United Nations participation in constitutional conferences was requested by representatives of the population (*inter alia*, Equatorial Guinea, 1968), but without result.

formal and final solution to a problem of self-determination. Had some such international co-operation been accepted in the discussion of the future of the six British West Indian dependent territories (now known as Associated States), the United Nations would probably not have questioned the self-determination process. Furthermore, if a better understanding of the options and of their consequences had existed, difficulties such as the secession of Anguilla or the strain between Barbuda and Antigua might have been avoided.

The United Nations has usually insisted—through its Committee of Twenty-Four—that before the final stages of self-determination are reached, a visiting mission go to the territory to familiarize itself with the local conditions and acquaint the people with the aims of the United Nations. This visit was generally refused by the administering Powers. But the United Nations has rarely specified that it should participate actively in the outlining and discussion of the options. It is suggested that in the future, any administering Power contemplating an exercise of self-determination for a small territory should bring in the United Nations at an early stage. The task of the United Nations would be facilitated if it could work out, on the one hand, a comprehensive list of the various theoretical possibilities open to mini-territories in search of a new status, and, on the other hand, a more limited but more detailed list of opportunities specially applicable to the territory in question.

It is not always easy to assess the manner in which private discussions on options proceed between the metropolitan Power and the representative of the dependent people concerned. Involvement by the United Nations might improve this process.

An interesting example of the discussion of options by representatives of the people themselves—so far without United Nations participation—is the examination of a list of possibilities included in the report of the Future Political Status Commission of the Congress of Micronesia.[4] This Committee was established in 1967, inter alia, to "present such range of possibilities and alternatives as may be open to Micronesians with respect to their choice of political status."[5]

Once the outline of the future status of the mini-territory takes shape, it becomes necessary to ascertain if it really corresponds to the wishes of the population. This may be achieved by a plebiscite, or by

[4] Interim Report from the Future Political Status Commission to the Congress of Micronesia, Fourth Regular Session, July 1968.

[5] The report attempts to identify all alternatives for a political status of the territory. From a geographical approach, three possibilities are examined: Micronesia may be expanded to include some other islands not presently in the Trust Territory: Guam, Nauru, American Samoa, the Cook Islands, the Gilbert and Ellice Islands and others; Micronesia may be divided; Micronesia may retain its present boundaries. From a political approach, the report examines four broad categories of political alternatives

elections of new legislative bodies (although in some cases the elections have preceded the constitutional discussions, and have served as a means of designating those who will participate in these discussions). It has been the traditional view of the United Nations that the best guarantee for the freedom of expression in such an exercise—and for the avoidance of subsequent controversy about this freedom—is United Nations supervision in some form or other.

As has been indicated above,[6] the United Nations was particularly active in plebiscites and elections in connexion with the attainment of independence of territories under the International Trusteeship System (Togoland under British administration, 1956; Togoland under French administration, 1958; Cameroons under British administration, 1959 and 1961; Western Samoa, 1961; Ruanda-Urundi, 1962). The first example of a dependent territory other than a Trust Territory where the United Nations supervised elections in connexion with self-determination was the Cook Islands in 1965. In 1968, a similar operation took place in Equatorial Guinea. In 1969, the act of self-determination in West New Guinea (West Irian) was supervised by the United Nations, in accordance with the 1962 Agreement between Indonesia and the Netherlands.

In general, however, the administering Powers (with the exception of New Zealand and Spain) have been most reluctant to accept any United Nations presence during elections or plebiscites bearing on a change of international status of a Non-Self-Governing Territory.[7] The United Nations General Assembly has indicated in a number of resolutions[8] that it considered United Nations supervision an important element in the assessment of the processes of self-determination. It seems likely that, in the future, the United Nations may have to participate in more and more of these operations. Therefore, it is desirable that a comprehensive survey and a critical analysis be made of its experience to date.

---

open to Micronesia: (a) independence; (b) a free associated state or protectorate status; (c) integration with a major power (Commonwealth status, unincorporated territory, incorporated territory); (d) remaining a Trust Territory. In addition, the report describes in some detail the status of some relevant territories: the Commonwealth of Puerto Rico, Western Samoa, the Cook Islands, the Philippines, Guam.

[6] See pp. 24-25.

[7] E.g., France, with reference to the referendum held on 19 March 1967 on French Somaliland. See also document A/AC.109/296 on the question of sending visiting missions.

[8] E.g., General Assembly resolution 2228 (XXI) of 20 December 1966, on French Somaliland: "Requests the administering Power, in consultation with the Secretary-General to make appropriate arrangements for a United Nations presence before, and supervision during, the holding of the referendum."

General Assembly resolution 2229 (XXI) of 20 December 1966 on Ifni and Spanish Sahara: "Invites the administering Power to determine . . . the procedures for holding a referendum under United Nations auspices. . . . To

II. Options open to small dependent territories emerging from dependent status

The question of options can be viewed from different angles, and although the choices according to these various aspects are interrelated and interdependent, the diversity of choice remains great.

From the point of view of self-government, the emergent small territory has a choice of a broad spectrum of possibilities, from full colonial status to complete self-government and independence. This choice concerns the internal machinery of government and administration. From the point of view of international status, there is a range of possibilities from strict colonial status to full independence, seen from the angle of how the territory is linked to the outside world. From the point of view of geography, the territory can evolve as an unchanged territorial unit, merge with other territorial units or put certain interests or activities in common with them; conversely, it may divide itself into parts which go each their own way. Finally, from the point of view of its participation in international organizations, there is a choice between solutions ranging from no relations at all with international organizations to full membership in all of them.

(a) *Self-government*

It has been contended that at any moment, and particularly at the time of choice, solutions are dictated not only by the wishes of the population, but by the preparedness and capability of that population to shoulder the burdens of self-government. It should not be forgotten, however, that the assessment of this capability varies greatly according to who makes it. The administering Power will often consider that the population is not adequately prepared, whereas the local *élite* will hold the opposite view.

At any rate, it is hard to conceive of a choice being made of accepting a continuation of an old colonial situation where there is no self-government at all. In situations where expatriates, mainly officials, still play a dominant rôle in legislative, executive, judicial and administrative affairs, the desire expressed by the population will usually be for a larger share of responsibility for the local population and a lesser rôle for the expatriates. Between the two extremes of no self-government at all and full self-government, there are many intermediate situations, some of which might commend themselves to the attention of the representatives of a people trying to exercise its right of self-determination. Certain fields such as foreign affairs, defence, police, finances, civil service, etc., may

provide all the necessary facilities to a United Nations mission so that it may be able to participate actively in the organization and holding of the referendum." Same language in resolution 2354 (XXII) of 19 December 1967.

provisionally be left out of the hands of the indigenous authorities; expatriate personnel may be retained as advisers in those and other fields. By definition, however, a territory "emerges" only when it opts for a degree of self government where the rôle of expatriate officials is reduced to a minimum or eliminated altogether. It should be noted also that on the road to self-government, any option is provisional and does not exclude a further evolution towards self-government. The gradual displacement of the expatriate officials and the widening of the fields of competence for the local people is often accomplished in stages.

As has been mentioned above, it is particularly important to ascertain which are the true wishes of the majority of the population when the option has been in favour of a limited degree of self-government only.

(b) *International status*

Dependent territories rely on the administering Power for their external relations. Even in cases of full internal self-government, the option can be to reserve external affairs to the metropolitan government. *A fortiori,* in cases of limited self-government, the international status of the territory will be of a dependent nature. Between such a situation and complete independence one can imagine a series of intermediate situations. A basic question on this subject, when options are discussed, is to evaluate to what extent the indigenous population can unilaterally modify the status whereby it leaves foreign relations in the hands of an outside power, and attain full independence without obstacles.

(c) *Geographical scope of the options*

In many instances, there is no question of either fragmentation or links with other territories. However, it has happened that when the question of choosing a new status arises, the territory wishes to split in parts, because it feels a lack of homogeneity, a lack of common aims, etc. Although fragmentation should not be encouraged, particularly in already very small territories, the question has to be seriously examined at the time of self-determination, lest early independence be marred by secessionist upheavals. On the other hand, it may be desirable for the options to include the possibility of links with other territories, distant or neighbouring. The association may be as close as total integration, or looser, such as federation, or limited to economic factors, such as common market or a customs union. Various alternatives exist, but at the time of choice, it is essential to make sure that the population of the small territory is ready and willing. Any closer union imposed from the outside, without proper preparation and acceptance by the population, is bound to get into difficulties, as has been demonstrated on many occasions.

(d) *Participation in international organizations*

Options varying from no participation in any international organization and membership in all of them have been enumerated above.[9]

B. FOR SMALL INDEPENDENT OR SEMI-INDEPENDENT TERRITORIES

The question of options arises, of course, basically for dependent territories emerging from colonial or semi-colonial status. However, no option is ever absolutely final. A small independent or semi-independent country may at some point consider new options, e.g., whether to merge with a larger unit or to federate with one, whether to apply for membership in international or regional organizations or withdraw from them, etc.

Being independent, the country can study the alternatives and take decisions all by itself, without any outside interference. By the same token, it can ask for advice, if it wishes to do so. A young small state may feel that it lacks all the information to take an enlightened decision of this sort. In that case, it would be quite in order for the United Nations to assist it, at its request, and provide information, documentation and expert advice. Such assistance might also alleviate the justified or unjustified feeling in the small territory that a decision might be taken under undue pressure from neighbouring countries or from the former administering Power. Although this is rather new ground, it might be recalled that in two instances, the United Nations stated its interest in options which might be exercised by small nations after self-determination. In the case of Western Samoa, which, after attaining independence in 1961, decided that it would not join the United Nations, the United Nations "expressed the hope that Western Samoa would be admitted to membership in the United Nations should it so desire."[10] In the case of the Cook Islands, the United Nations noted that the people of these islands had the control of their internal affairs and of their future, and "reaffirmed the responsibility of the United Nations, under General Assembly resolution 1514 (XV) to assist the people of the Cook Islands in the eventual achievement of full independence, if they so wish, at a future date."[11]

The idea of residual responsibilities of the United Nations after self-determination has been raised occasionally in the General Assembly.[12]

[9] See pp. 118 *et seq.*
[10] General Assembly resolution 1626 (XVI) of 18 October 1961.
[11] General Assembly resolution 2064 (XX) of 16 December 1965.
[12] On 10 October 1967, the representative of Jamaica stated: "Since the 19th regular session of the General Assembly, Jamaica has been calling attention to the need for the United Nations to have some residual rôle to play in the future of those Territories which, having exercised their right of self-determination in accordance with resolution *1541* (XV), have chosen association with another State" (A/PV.1584, p. 17).

CHAPTER TWO

CONFERENCES ON PROBLEMS OF SMALL STATES

In the limited context of decolonization, it has been proposed[1] that the possibility be considered of "convening, under the auspices of the United Nations, a conference of representatives of those small [dependent] territories. Such a conference would enable the representatives of those peoples to bring out their problems and to state their desires, to propose pertinent solutions on the basis of which the United Nations could work out a broad programme of action, with a view to helping to solve the problems posed by the existence of the so-called small territories, whose people also have the right to self-determination and independence."

Although this idea was barely discussed, the General Assembly included in its 1967 resolution on decolonization[2] a paragraph 19 requesting the Committee of Twenty-Four "to consider and submit recommendations to the General Assembly at its twenty-third session regarding the holding early in 1969 of a special conference of representatives of colonial peoples for the purpose, *inter alia*, of considering the most effective means by which the international community can intensify its assistance to them in their effort to achieve self-determination, freedom and independence."

As can be seen from the text, this proposal is not confined to small territories, but is related more generally to "colonial peoples." As is well known, however, the great majority of the remaining colonial territories are at present the small ones.

In its 1968 report to the General Assembly,[3] the Special Committee of Twenty-Four stated that it had "noted that the year 1970 would be the tenth anniversary of the adoption of the Declaration on the Granting of Independence to Colonial Countries and Peoples, as well as the twenty-fifth anniversary of the establishment of the United Nations . . ." and suggested "that the General Assembly should authorize the organization of a special programme of activities in connexion with the tenth anniversary of the adoption of the Declaration and that in the context of that programme consideration might be given to the holding of a conference as envisaged in operative paragraph 19 of General Assembly resolution 2326 (XXII) together with any other proposals that may be made in connexion with that programme."

The idea of having some sort of conference at which problems of

---

[1] By Yugoslavia in the General Assembly 1966 (A/PV.1490, 12 December 1966, p. 86) and in the Committee of Twenty-Four in 1967 (A/AC.109/PV.487, 15 February 1967, p. 11).

[2] General Assembly resolution 2326 (XXII), 16 December 1967.

[3] A/7200 (Part I), paras. 96-99.

small states and territories would be thrashed out, mainly but not exclusively by representatives of these small countries, is an interesting and fruitful one, especially if it is not restricted to problems of self-determination of dependent territories. It is, therefore, suggested that consideration be given to the idea of organizing a conference focusing on smallness rather than on decolonization. There are different aspects to that idea.

First of all, there is the idea of convening representatives of the small dependent territories, preferably with the co-operation of the administering Powers concerned, and having them discuss the problems of smallness as it affects self-determination.

Secondly, a discussion of the problems of smallness after self-determination is suggested.

Finally, thought might be given to the examination of the problems of smallness on a regional basis.

Whether there should be one conference or more than one is a matter for discussion. However, a general conference could be broken down into various committees, one examining the problems of self-determination of small dependent territories, another the political and economic problems of independent or semi-independent states and territories, and a third the regional approach as a solution to problems of smallness.

If a conference or conferences on problems of small states and territories could be called under the auspices of the United Nations, it would serve a very useful purpose. But if the United Nations cannot convene such a conference, it is to be hoped that something along the same lines could be organized by private sources, a foundation, a university, etc. The participants should be selected, as far as possible, from among the people directly concerned; in other words, they should represent the small states and territories concerned. In order to avoid certain difficulties, however, it might be preferable to invite the participants in their personal capacity, either upon nomination by their government or according to more complex arrangements. It is also essential to invite outsiders, who could make a contribution because of special experience in the field, in administrative or regional bodies or in institutions of higher learning.

The conference should be thoroughly prepared, with papers contributed by eminent personalities representing various viewpoints and disciplines. Participants should receive them well in advance so that active preliminary discussion can take place locally, on a formal or informal basis, in the territories themselves.

The main aim of the conference would be to afford a confrontation of ideas and a contact among people responsible, involved or interested in aspects of political smallness: the problems of self-determination; the problems of the choice of a new status; the alternatives to independence;

the difficulties of independence; the economic, public administration, social and educational aspects of smallness; the expectations of the small territories; their participation in international life and co-operation; the possibilities and modalities of international assistance, etc.

Such a confrontation has never taken place. Yet a week of carefully prepared discussion would probably be a revelation for the participants, and might constitute a serious step forward in the formulation of new productive ideas.

CHAPTER THREE

GUARANTEES FOR SECURITY AND PROTECTION

A look at the map shows that military bases or communications installations of value to big countries or to military alliances or blocs are often located in mini-territories who are still dependencies of a colonial Power.

Ironically enough, when the mini-territory has become, or is likely to become, independent, and when because of political, strategic or technical considerations, the military base or installation has lost its value for the former colonial Power and there is a question of dismantling it, the economy of the mini-state appears sometimes to be threatened. Efforts are then made by the mini-state to delay the closing of the military base or to phase it out over a long period so as to facilitate the reconversion of the life of the territory. These situations are consequences of the colonial régime under which the small territories had found themselves at some time or other.

In other cases, independent mini-states may experience a feeling of insecurity because of their proximity to larger and more powerful neighbours, or because they feel trapped in the currents of power politics. Some will resign themselves to a position of complete vulnerability, others will enter into defence alliances or protection arrangements with a neighbour or neighbours, foreign powers, regional groups, blocs, etc.

Some mini-states may attempt to maintain some kind of national military apparatus. But the development and maintenance of adequate national armed forces and military installations are generally beyond the physical and financial capacity of mini-states. As one author has stated, "given defence considerations alone, the economic burdens of safe-guarding independence are proportionately far heavier in a small than in a large country—*ceteris paribus*."[1]

---

[1] *Economic Consequences of the Size of Nations*, edited by E. A. G. Robinson, pp. 26-27 ("Economic growth of small nations," by S. Kuznets).

However,

> the burdens may be so unequal that alliances may prove to be in the long run the indispensable prerequisite for survival: and such alliances can be more valuable to the small states than the larger—thus offsetting the original disadvantage of small size.[2]

There are examples of relatively small states which are maintaining their independence without any military establishment and without any military alliance. Most mini-states simply cannot afford a defence establishment of their own; this does not mean that they have necessarily to rely on the protection of another state or of a military bloc. They may put the fate of their territorial integrity in the hands of the international community.

By avoiding the uneconomic use of resources for external security purposes, by foregoing an important theoretical manifestation of their sovereignty, those mini-states make in a certain sense a modest contribution to the concept of a world order less dependent on the use of force, particularly, if they are willing to forgo entering into military alliances and accepting the establishment of bases on their territory.

When a mini-state maintains no defence establishment of any kind, enters into no military alliance and does not put its territory at the disposal of another country for military purposes, it contributes somehow to the relaxation of international tensions and to general disarmament, and is entitled to a special measure of protection from the international community. If a number of mini-states, Members or non-Members of the United Nations, express such a desire, could the United Nations not examine the question of giving them special and effective international guarantees against external aggression or threat of aggression? This may be less difficult to achieve than more ambitious schemes in the field of peace and security, because the mini-states are further removed from power politics. This might be an interesting, if modest, experience in collective security, and if it succeeds, mini-states would have helped the United Nations in making some progress in the achievement of one of the fundamental purposes of the Charter.

In a different context, it may be noted that the United Nations has already become involved in the security of mini-states; it has actively intervened in Cyprus, and has expressed concern at the possible threat to the territorial integrity and sovereignty of Basutoland (now Lesotho), Bechuanaland (now Botswana) and Swaziland.[3]

---

[2] *Ibid.*, pp. 234 *et seq.* ("The size of the nation and the cost of administration," by E.A.G. Robinson.)

[3] General Assembly resolution 2134 (XXI) of 29 September 1966.

CHAPTER FOUR

CONVENTIONAL INTERNATIONAL ASSISTANCE

In order to qualify for assistance from the United Nations Development Programme, the mini-states (or the Power administering dependent mini-territories) need only be a Member of either the United Nations or one of the specialized agencies.

Small territories do benefit from the United Nations Development Programme. Recent figures show that for the 1967-68 approved country programmes of Technical Assistance, out of 131 beneficiary countries, 37 had a population of a million or less.[1] As far as the Special Fund component of UNDP is concerned, out of 105 beneficiary countries and territories, 13 had a population of under one million.[2]

The participation of the small territories can better be judged by the following table (regional and interregional programmes and projects are not included here, although some of them comprise small territories):

TECHNICAL ASSISTANCE APPROVED PROGRAMME FOR 1967-68
[Country programmes only (experts, fellowships and equipment)]

	Countries	Population	Total Cost	%	Assistance per inhabitant
Technical Assistance total	131	1,666,300,000	$93,739,140	100	$0.056
T.A. mini-territories	37	10,332,000	$ 6,513,071	7	$0.630

SPECIAL FUND COUNTRY PROJECTS AS OF 30 JUNE 1968

	Countries	Population	Projects	Governing Council earmarkings	%	Assistance per inhabitant
Special Fund total	105	1,732,500,000	866	$818,018,787	100	$0.472
Special Fund mini-territories	13	6,231,000	42	$35,384,418	4.3	$5.670

[1] DP/L.67/Add.1, of 30 April 1968. These 37 are: Antigua, Bahamas,

Insofar as it is meaningful to compare amounts of international aid *per capita* in different countries, the small territories get eleven to twelve times more assistance than the average country in each programme.

However, in many cases this assistance in absolute value is extremely low (for example, Wallis and Futuna have an approved 1967-68 technical assistance programme of one 3-month fellowship amounting to $800; the Bahamas, a programme of five expert-months amounting to $7,650). Whether such small amounts of assistance can make a real impact on the country concerned remains to be seen. It may be worthwhile to evaluate critically on the spot the usefulness of these small programmes, and if necessary consider the possibility of amending the rules and practices of assistance relating to very small territories.

Technical assistance to mini-territories is sometimes limited by the 12½ per cent or 15 per cent that these territories must pay towards local operating cost. It seems that many small territories cannot afford this burden, and thought might be given to establishing a sliding scale for these contributions.

A greater degree of regionalization might be applied in areas where many small territories are relatively close to each other. The United Nations Development Programme has already endorsed the idea of regionalization, and has two regional representatives in the Pacific and the Caribbean areas, located respectively in Western Samoa and Trinidad. When an expert is sent to a small territory, he should be offered systematically to neighbouring small territories, wherever appropriate. Whenever a project is contemplated for a very small territory, thought should be given to expanding it to other small territories, if at all possible. In this way, some projects which might be too small to be of interest to the Development Programme might acquire a more practical value. The United Nations Development Programme should progressively constitute a corps of specialists in practical problems of smallness who would be used regionally.

In the future, more and more mini-states and mini-territories will be knocking at the door of the United Nations Development Programme. It is to be hoped that the administrators of this programme will bear in mind the particular needs and merits of very small territories in their search for

---

Barbados, Botswana, British Honduras, Comoro Islands, Congo (Brazzaville), Cyprus, Dominica, Fiji, French Somaliland, Gabon, The Gambia, Gilbert and Ellice Islands, Grand Cayman Island, Grenada, Guyana, Kuwait, Lesotho, Maldive Islands, Malta, Mauritius, Montserrat, Netherlands Antilles, New Hebrides, Seychelles, Solomon Islands, St. Kitts, St. Lucia, St. Vincent, Surinam, Swaziland, Tonga, Tortola (British Virgin Islands), Trinidad and Tobago, Wallis and Futuna, Western Samoa.

[2] DP/SF/Reports Series B, No. 6. These 13 are: Botwana, British Solomon Islands, Congo (Brazzaville), Fiji, Gabon, Guyana, Iceland, Kuwait, Malta, Mauritius, Surinam, Swaziland, Trinidad and Tobago.

development. In view of the share the small territories already receive, it is doubtful that considerably larger amounts will be set aside for them, unless there is a marked over-all increase in development funds available. Any further attempt to seek privileged treatment for small territories might antagonize the larger recipients of international aid. Therefore, if a case can be made about the fact that mini-states and mini-territories deserve special solicitude and services from the international community, it would be more realistic to think in terms of a special programme or a special fund which would supplement the conventional international assistance already available and the assistance obtained on a bilateral basis.

CHAPTER FIVE

SPECIAL UNITED NATIONS SERVICES AND ASSISTANCE TO VERY SMALL STATES AND TERRITORIES

In examining the question of possible special assistance by the United Nations to very small states and territories, it is necessary to keep in mind that their international status varies greatly: some are independent and Members of the United Nations, others independent and not Members of the United Nations, others semi-independent with certain limitations on their foreign relations, others partly autonomous but entirely dependent in respect to their external relations, etc.

Rather than lumping these various categories together and examining what new ideas of assistance could be applied to them, it might be more fruitful to select first one category for the purpose of looking into the possible special aid the United Nations can provide. As a second step, one could examine whether any scheme envisaged for these territories could also be applied, *mutatis mutandis,* to other categories.

The group selected for this examination includes the independent mini-states which are not full Members of the Organization, and those semi-independent mini-states which have some say in their foreign relations, but are not Members of the United Nations.

The reason for this choice is that the mini-states which are Members of the United Nations have—theoretically, at least—all the privileges and possibilities of other Member States, and—theoretically again—should have no special problems of contact with the outside world, or of access to international life and international co-operation (in fact, however, this is not entirely true. As has been indicated in other parts of this study, even Members of the United Nations, when they are very small and have limited resources, have their difficulties in enjoying all the advantages of full membership of the United Nations). On the other hand, those territories which are still dependent rely entirely on their administering Powers for their relations with the outside world. Moreover, they have usually not yet made a decision on self-determination.

What are the international wishes of a small state which decides that it cannot afford, or should not apply for, full membership in the United Nations?

First of all, of course, is a desire for security, for protection against external threat or use of force. It has already been suggested above that very small states which have no bilateral military arrangements or bases on their territory might receive special guarantees from the United Nations.

Another major wish of these territories is to have the possibility of making their voice heard in the international community whenever they feel that a subject of direct interest to them is at stake, or to which they feel they can make a contribution.

Apart from the desire to feel accepted, to feel part of the international community, the small state wishes to be in a position to benefit from all forms of international co-operation, mainly as a beneficiary, but also, if possible, as a donor.

The normal way to achieve such aims is for states to have in the country a ministry for external relations, and outside the country a net of embassies and permanent missions to the international organizations. The obvious way for a small country limited by its human and financial resources is to reduce the size of its foreign ministry, maintain only a few essential embassies, limit its membership to a few international organizations and cut to the bone its personnel to permanent missions abroad. The next economy move is to be represented abroad and in international organizations by another country.

While this last procedure is obviously not satisfactory, the representation in international organizations by a skeleton staff, or an intermittent mission, is not entirely acceptable either. International activities have become so numerous and complicated, documentation is so abundant and procedures so intricate, that one person is incapable of following everything regularly.

It has been suggested in various quarters that a link between the outside world, namely, the international organizations, and the mini-states be provided in some way by the United Nations Secretariat.

At the 22nd session of the General Assembly, the representative of Jamaica mentioned this idea without going into detail. He stated:

> There are also those small states, economically not viable, which would choose full independence if they could. It should not be beyond the capacity of the United Nations to devise means of linking them to this Organization in order to ensure that the exercise of their right does not lead them to continuing or eventual poverty. Specifically it would not be amiss, for the General

Assembly to recommend that a section of the Secretariat should devote itself exclusively to the interests of small territories which might elect to exercise that right. This special section could provide technical and administrative assistance where needed.[1]

This idea was also mentioned by some outsiders.[2]

Among the various ideas concerning the relations of mini-states with the United Nations and their respective rôles, this idea seems to be among the most fruitful ones.

What could a Secretariat section do for non-Member mini-states?

Its first function could be as a liaison and information centre for all the non-Member mini-states which would like to use these services. It would provide at no cost to the mini-states the desired link with the international organization. The unit would be a clearing house for United Nations documentation. It would regularly and automatically send to the non-Member mini-states general information about the activities of the United Nations (for example, the weekly summary of events put out by the Office of Public Information), and whatever more specialized documentation it believed the mini-state would be interested in, according to its specific circumstances. It would furnish any information about the activities of the United Nations and the United Nations family of organizations which the mini-states would request. Regular relations between the mini-states and the unit would generate a desire to be better informed about international activities and would soon result in the unit having a clearer idea as to what was important for the mini-state. This function may seem restricted and limited in scope and importance; in fact, howover, for a small country which has no representation or observer's post in New York, it is extremely difficult to keep abreast of what goes on in the United Nations and the agencies, and of what may be of direct interest to the country. It is extremely difficult to know to whom to write and what to request, and only by establishing a central point in the United Nations Secretariat can these difficulties be overcome. Once such a link existed, it would be possible for the mini-state to make informed decisions about the advisability of sending an occasional observer to United Nations meetings, or to ask to be heard on special matters.

The unit would also serve as a centre of information and assistance for all activities and requests relating to the United Nations Development Programme, particularly if the mini-state concerned were not adequately covered by an office of a Resident Representative.

It would also provide a physical location for officials of small states who were passing through New York, on United Nations business or otherwise. It would provide them with facilities such as secretarial

---

[1] A/PV.1584, p. 17, 10 October 1967.
[2] Patricia W. Blair, *The Ministate Dilemma,* p. 65, referring to proposals made by Professor R. Fisher.

services, access to documentation, etc. In other words, the unit would physically run a joint observer's office to the United Nations for as many small non-Member states as would require the service, ensuring office facilities, documentation, despatch of documents and correspondence, etc.

A very important, but more delicate function would be that of adviser to the small states on any question they may wish to raise. The unit would to some extent become a permanent study bureau on mini-state affairs, at the disposal of these states. Any question would not necessarily receive a substantive answer, but whenever the latter was not possible, indications would be given as to how and where to find the answer. Many questions will be in the economic and social fields. However, questions in the political field should not be excluded. Advice could be given in the fields of public administration, constitutional law or international relations. There may be questions which are impossible to answer without taking a partisan position—these should be avoided. In such cases, the unit should refrain from getting involved beyond a certain point.

The unit should also promote further studies and seminars, within the United Nations and without, on practical and theoretical problems of smallness.

It is difficult to anticipate exactly the scope of activity of the unit in question. It may be preferable to leave its terms of reference relatively vague and see what is the character of business it will be called upon to transact. Only an experimental use of such a new and unorthodox institution will reveal whether it serves its purpose or not.

It may be argued that such a scheme smacks of United Nations neocolonialism or paternalism *vis-à-vis* the mini-states. This is not true. Any mini-state using the services of the special unit would do it only when it wished to do so. Furthermore, it could do what it wanted with the documentation or advice received, or ignore it altogether.

Some private soundings seem to indicate that such a system would be welcome to a number of non-Member mini-states. As a matter of fact, certain representatives of small Member States have commented that had such a system existed at the time of their admission, they might have postponed, temporarily or indefinitely, their membership application. The establishment of such a unit might therefore reduce the pressure on newly independent mini-states to ask for immediate membership in the United Nations.

The initiative of contacting the mini-states in order to activate the unit, should come from the Secretary-General or the Secretariat, in order to explain what services are available and to ask whether the state is interested. This can be done by correspondence. If it can be followed by a visit *in loco,* so much the better.

Such services would not require a large staff and hence would not impose much of a financial burden on the Organization. Action would consist mainly of gathering and sending existing documents, obtaining from the various sections in the Secretariat or the specialized agencies readily available information, or initiating action or research in other parts of the Secretariat. For the special unit, it would generally be more a question of serving as a focal point or clearing house rather than of taking substantive action (although this may occasionally be necessary). A very small staff having access to all the resources of the Secretariat and other United Nations organizations would suffice.

The question arises as to whether, if such a unit is established, its use should be restricted to non-Member states, or whether it could be expanded to serve certain needs of Member mini-states and dependent mini-territories.

As far as Member mini-states are concerned (assuming for instance that they are defined as Member States with a population of one million or less), the unit could be of considerable assistance to those which cannot afford to maintain an adequately staffed permanent delegation in New York. The unit could easily provide joint physical facilities for a number of Member mini-states: office, documentation, correspondence. The mini-state might even lack permanently stationed national personnel, but temporary national delegates and visitors could use the office as the need arose. The unit might also be asked to facilitate research and to perform for the mini-state various actions which are normally taken by a permanent mission.

Unlike non-Member states, for which the services would be free, the Member mini-state would have to pay a suitable charge for use of the Secretariat unit. The more states that used this office, the lower the charge would be.

As far as dependent mini-territories are concerned, if the administering Power delegates to them some aspects of foreign relations, they could, with the consent of the administering Power, make similar use of the Secretariat unit. In fact, this experience would constitute good training for the period following self-determination. In such a case, a charge for the services of the Secretariat unit would also be made payable by the administering Power.

The scheme described above should be introduced in stages: first for a few non-Member mini-states, then for others; first for limited services, then for more numerous functions. If the scheme were successful, a similar office at the United Nations Headquarters might be set up in Geneva, concentrating on matters relating to specialized agencies in Europe. It is even possible to envision such an office in certain important capitals where most mini-Members have no representation, but where they may wish to have a non-diplomatic representation for certain specific purposes.

In the long run, a problem may arise concerning the staff attached to the special unit or to its branches. Will there be a point at which it will lose its international character because it will "seek or receive instructions" from a government or an authority external to the United Nations? This loss would certainly not occur at the beginning of the operation, and would arise at a later stage only in exceptional cases. A solution might be to consider some of the staff members of the unit as personnel of the new "OPEX" type, assisting directly all the mini-states concerned.

The general scheme of special services for mini-states requires no amendment of the Charter (as would be required by the creation of an associated status, weighted voting, joint membership, etc.). A General Assembly resolution would suffice, authorizing the Secretary-General to proceed on an experimental basis along the lines discussed above, and, if need be, with certain additional safeguards to be worked out by a committee established by the General Assembly or by the Secretary-General. Even without formal General Assembly action, the Secretary-General could initiate such action, on a provisional basis and on a modest scale. After a year or two, the scheme should be reviewed with a view to improve, expand or discontinue it.

ANNEX

STATISTICAL TYPOLOGY OF MICRO-STATES AND TERRITORIES[1] TOWARDS A DEFINITION OF A MICRO-STATE

People are fascinated by picturesque little places such as Liechtenstein and San Marino, and enough stamp collectors take their sovereignty seriously to keep their post offices in business. For the political scientist, however, these small entities are a reminder of the richness and multiplicity of polities and of the difficulties of defining sovereignty in the last third of the twentieth century. What is a micro-state? By what criteria is a territory to be considered "micro?" At what point, if any, must it cease to be considered a state? What, other than the accidents of history and geography, determines the difference between such entities as the Isle of Man, with its own thousand-year-old Parliament, and the Isle of Wight, which has no more status than being part of Hampshire? Does location play as important a rôle as size in determining identity and viability?

A. CRITERIA FOR DETERMINING MICRO-TERRITORIES

The first problem is to define what classifies a territory as "micro." Presumably, we are interested in those very small places which have administrative and legal systems perceived to be common only to themselves. They may be politically independent or not; they may even be overseas departments or provinces whose integration with the metropole is meaningful or is not. We start, however, with all entities whose legal, geographical, cultural or economic characteristics place them as separate units in the United Nations Demographic Yearbooks. This method of selection is not a judgement on constitutional arrangements; indeed, later on we will discuss our sample according to legal status. At the moment, however, we are concentrating only on criteria for determining "micro."

[1] This annex has been contributed by Professor Charles L. Taylor, World Data Analysis Program, Yale University.

Micro-states have most often been defined in terms of population. States wtih populations less than 100,000 or 300,000 or 1,000,000 or whatever were considered "micro." The arbitrariness of the cut-off point is not accidental. If the territories of the world are plotted into a frequency distribution by population size (i.e., in such a way that the number of territories for each category of population size is shown), the curve on the lower end of the distribution does not turn downward at any point (see Figure 1). In other words, no matter what point along the distribution one chooses, there are always more territories per unit of size to the left than to the right. Or, to put it another way, the smaller the size of territory, the more of them exist.[2] Moreover, there is no obvious break between larger and smaller at any point in the distribution. The upswings in the curves in Figure 1 cannot be used as magic identifiers of micro-territories, since their locations depend entirely upon the size interval chosen. Compare Figure 1a, 1b, and 1c, which use intervals of ten million, one-half million and one thousand, respectively.[3]

Thresholds in terms of area and economic size must also be arbitrary. The frequency distributions for total area, gross national product and aggregate energy consumption look very much like those for population. There are more smaller states, no matter what the variable and almost no matter at what point on the scale one chooses; moreover, as with population, there are no clear cut-off points within the distributions. The exception to these generalizations is in the "left tail" of the two economic size variables where, if the intervals are small enough, there is a slight downward turn on the left side of the distribution (see Figure 2). The margins of error in the data, however, are such as to prevent us from interpreting these aberrations.

Another way to define micro-territories is by the use of medians, quartiles and deciles. A median is that point which separates all the cases into two halves; quartiles divide them into equal fourths, and deciles into equal tenths. Since we have populations for 222 territories, we find the median population by subtracting the value for the 111th territory from that of the 112th, dividing the result by two and adding this quotient to the original value for the 111th territory. (If the cases had been odd in number, we would simply have taken the value of the middle one.) The

[2] This has been true historically. Evidence from ancient times as well as data for 1938, 1957 and 1967 show the distribution of territories by population to be positively skewed, sufficiently, in fact, for their logarithms to the base 10 to approach normality of distribution. See Bruce M. Russett, "Is There a Long-Run Trend Toward Concentration in the International System?", *Comparative Political Studies*, I, 1(April, 1968), pp. 103-122.

[3] Data on size refer to 1965 and come from the United Nations Statistical Office's *Demographic Yearbook, 1966, Statistical Yearbook, 1966* and *Yearbook of National Account Statistics, 1965* and from various country studies and reports.

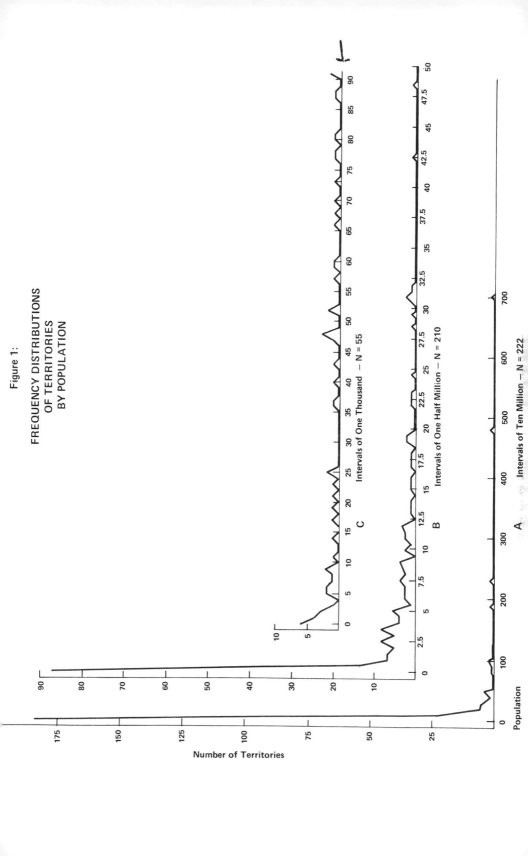

Figure 1:

FREQUENCY DISTRIBUTIONS
OF TERRITORIES
BY POPULATION

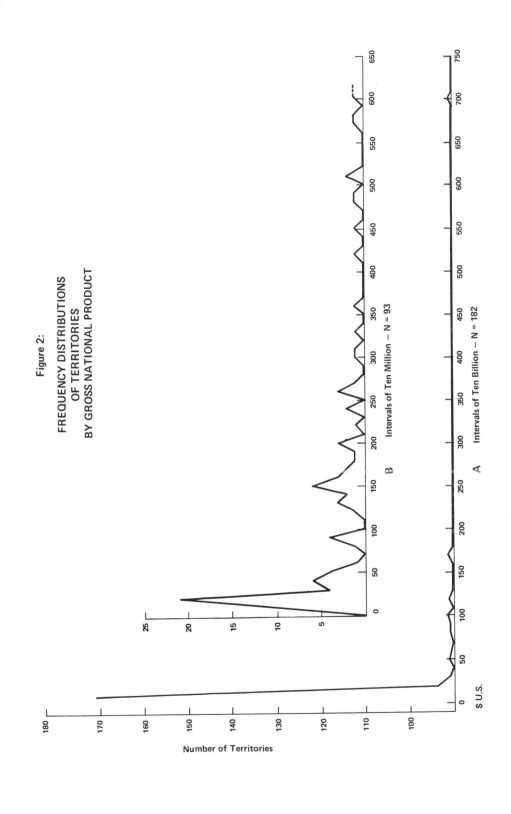

Figure 2:

FREQUENCY DISTRIBUTIONS
OF TERRITORIES
BY GROSS NATIONAL PRODUCT

median value for 1966 populations was 1,647,000, a figure by which one might wish to delimit small territories, but one perhaps a little large for micro-territories. The 22 territories in the first decile have populations up to 9,000, and the 56 territories in the first quartile range upward to 96,000. Similar statistics for the other three variables are as follows:

Variable	Median	First quartile	First decile	Unit
area (n = 222)	79,000	1,102	135	square kilometres
GNP (n = 182)	572	51	12	million $US
energy con-sumption · (n = 163)	.75	.12	.05	million metric tons—coal equivalents ·

Once again, it is clear that the use of one's head is necessary in determining the limits of micro-territories; whatever the threshold chosen, it will be an arbitrary one, tempered only by the theoretical criteria which are used in its determination.

Thus far, we have taken each of the variables separately; however, this approach has its difficulties. Is Hong Kong to be a micro-state because it has only 1,000 square kilometres of land area? One could just as well call it a more "normal" state, because it does have a population of 3,804,000 and a GNP of $1,600 million (well above the world median in each case). Is Namibia (South West Africa), with its 824,300 sq. km. but only 574,000 people, large or small? (For better comparison, the ranges of these variables are: population, 87—700,000,000 people; area, less than one-half square kilometre to 22,402,200 sq. km.; GNP, less than one-half million US dollars to $695.5 billion).

It is possible to employ all three dimensions simultaneously in separating micro-territories from the others in the world. If we take the 181 territories for which we have GNP, population and area,[4] we can imagine each at some point in a cube whose edges are measured by standardized scores for the three variables. Measures are standardized in order to weight each variable equally. Any other weighting scheme could be used, but equal weights seem reasonable for present purposes (see Figure 3). Each territory-point is obviously a specific distance from every other point. This distance can be measured by

[4] Of the 41 territories not included because of unknown economic size, 19 were places with less than 100,000 people, and 20 had less than 2,000 sq. km. No particular kind of micro-territory appeared to be consistently excluded, however. Missing are small states of Europe and North America, as well as islands of the Pacific and city states of North Africa (see footnote 6).

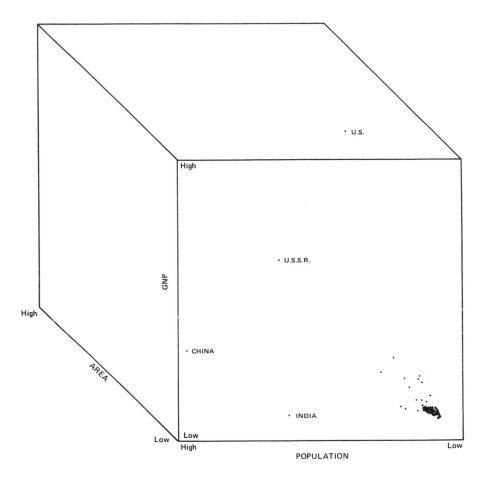

Figure 3:

LOCATION OF 181 TERRITORIES BY SIZE

$$d(x, y) = \sqrt{\sum_{i=1}^{3} (x_i - y_i)^2}$$

where x = the first country, y = the second and i refers to the variable; i.e., the distance between country x and country y is the square root of the sum of the squares of their distances measured on each of the three variables separately. If the average distance from each point to all other points were exactly the same, the points would then be scattered randomly throughout the cube, and no grouping of territories according to size would be possible. As it is, the points are clustered in one corner of the cube. In fact, they are more highly concentrated in the bottom right front corner than the scale of Figure 3 allows to be shown; six dots there represent ties of 125 countries. If this small section of the cube were to be blown up to size of the full cube, there would be a similar dispersion of fewer countries in the new cube. The iterative "blowing up" of the densest section of each new cube could continue to produce cubes with distributions more or less like the one shown until we ran out of countries. This follows from the nature of the three separate frequency distributions discussed earlier; there are always more countries which are smaller per unit of size.

If a cluster is made up of points whose distances among themselves are small as compared with their distances to points in other clusters (i.e., in our case, of territories similar in combined population, GNP and area), it would at first appear that we are limited to saying that only one cluster exists, and that its size depends upon our choice of cut-off points. In fact, by one method of clustering, this is exactly what happens. We can find an index of cohesion by summing up all distances and dividing by n:

$$C = \frac{\sum d(x, y)}{n}$$

where n = number of total observations (or points).
If this score is equal to or less than a predetermined threshold, the territories may be considered one cluster. If the score is greater than the threshold, however, the most "offensive" territory, i.e., the one whose average of distances to all other territories is greatest, is dropped from the cluster. A new cohesion score is found on n-1, and the process is continued until the cohesion score is equal to or less than the threshold. Once the first cluster is found, the distances among all of the previously discarded points form a new matrix to test for new clusters. With data of our kind, there are no second clusters when most thresholds are used, but the size and number of clusters depend entirely upon the particular threshold chosen. Clustering, therefore, is not an automatic way to categorize states by size without the use of any theoretical criteria.

A procedure of hierarchical clustering, proposed by Stephen C.

Johnson, seems more appropriate for our data.[5] By this method is constructed a hierarchy or tree of clusterings, ranging from one in which each of the points (territories) is considered a cluster by itself to one in which all 181 points (territories) are grouped into one single cluster. Unlike the first method described, in which every point was assumed to be in one cluster unless "proven" otherwise, the Johnson method begins by assuming each to be in a cluster by itself. Then, in searching a table that gives distances from every point to every other point, it finds the smallest non-zero entry and clusters the two points which this smallest distance connects, i.e., the two territories most alike in terms of their combinations of population, GNP and area. For example, if the distances (similarities) of x, y and z are as follows:

	x	y	z
x	0	3	5
y	3	0	4
z	5	4	0

then x and y would be clustered (zero entries are ignored, since if the distance between two points is zero, they are in the same place and are in fact the same point, i.e., $d(x,y) = 0$ is the same as $x = y$). The total number of points is then effectively reduced by one, and a new matrix of distances is formed. The distance from the new cluster to other points (or clusters) is defined as the greater of the distances from the points making up the cluster or

$$d([x, y],z) = \max [d(x, z), d(y, z)]$$

when x and y are the points in the new cluster and z is any third point (or previously formed cluster). In our example, the matrix—reduced by one—is

	x-y	z
x-y	0	5
z	5	0

Again, the matrix is searched for the smallest non-zero entry and another

[5] Stephen C. Johnson (Bell Telephone Laboratories), "Hierarchical Clustering Schemes," *Psychometrika*, XXXII, 3 (September, 1967), pp. 241-254. The subject of clustering is one on which there is no general agreement among statisticians. Results depend entirely upon the algorithm. For surveys of various methods, see Geoffrey H. Ball (Stanford Research Institute), "Data Analysis in the Social Sciences: What About the Details?", American Federation of Information Processing Societies Conference Proceedings, Fall Joint Computer Conference, XXVII (1965), pp. 533-559, and Ronald E. Frank and Paul E. Green, "Numerical Taxonomy in Marketing Analysis: A Review Article," *Journal of Market Research*, V (February, 1968), pp. 83-98.

cluster is formed. The process continues until all points are in one cluster (rather rapidly accomplished, of course, in our example):

where brackets indicate clustering and the numbers indicate the value of the cluster or distance at which the cluster occurred.

The value assigned to each of these clusterings, or cross-sections of the tree, represents the diameter of the largest cluster at that level. (This conclusion follows from the use of the maximum distance in relating a cluster to a third point or cluster). At the first level this value is zero, since none of the points is clustered. The value grows until finally it is the distance between the two most remote points. Again we must make a decision as to the cross-section of the tree in which we are really interested. If we choose a lower value, we will get more but smaller and more homogeneous clusters; if we choose a higher one, we will get fewer but larger and more heterogeneous clusters. The added advantages of the hierarchical method, however, are that we can think in terms of sub-clusters and super-clusters, and that we can be very precise as to when the clustering occurs.

Tables IX and X reproduce the top part of the hierarchy for the 181 territories. In Table IX the territories are listed as they are clustered at a value of 1.0 (stated in terms of the z scores used to standardize the variables). As in the example above, brackets to the right of the listing show subsequent clusterings, and numbers below indicate the value of these clusterings. All of the 181 form one cluster at the value of 13.6 (the distance in z scores from the largest to the smallest territory). Table X begins with a much lower value (0.03) than Table IX. In fact, it ends before the latter begins; the 74 territories that cluster at 0.06 are only a part of the first cluster of Table IX.

It seems reasonable to term the 74 territories in Table X micro-territories.[6] The list tends to "fit" one's intuitive notion of what they are. Their areas range up to 142,822 sq. km.; their GNP's, to $1,583 million; their populations, to 2,928,000. There are other territories with smaller areas,

---

[6] Some rather obvious micro-territories are excluded from this list for lack of economic data necessary for the clustering. Territories with less than 500,000 people missing from Tables IX and X include: Andorra, Bonin Islands, British Antarctic Territory, Canton and Enderbury, Ceuta, Channel Islands, Christmas Island, Cocos (Keeling) Islands, Faroe Islands, French Southern and Antarctic Territories, Greenland, Ifni, Isle of Man, Johnston Island, Maldive Islands, Melilla, Midway Island, Norfolk Island, Spanish North Africa, Spanish Sahara, Trucial Oman, Wake Island.

TABLE I — HIERARCHICAL CLUSTERING OF 181 COUNTRIES
(beginning with value of 1.0 and ending with value of 13.6)

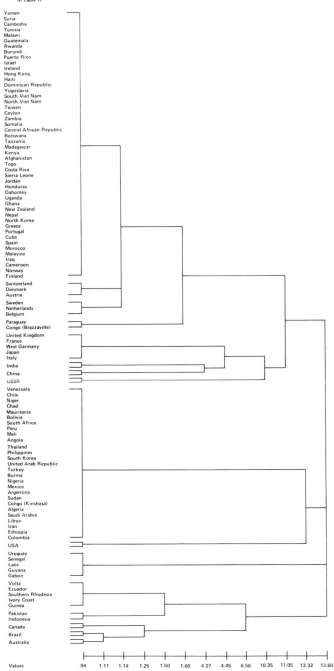

TABLE II – HIERARCHICAL CLUSTERING OF 74 TERRITORIES
(beginning with value of 0.03 and ending with value of 0.06)

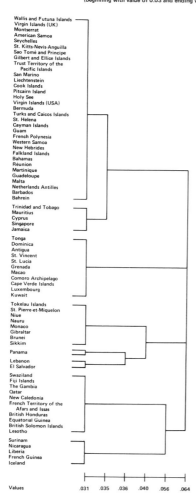

| Values | .031 | .035 | .036 | .040 | .056 | .064 |

less wealth and fewer people. To take an earlier example, Hong Kong has a much smaller area but much greater wealth and population. Yet these 74 territories are tiny in the sense that *the particular configurations of their three size variables taken together make them so.* Scores for the other territories on one, two or three variables were much higher.

There are some distinctions among the micro-territories, however. Lebanon and El Salvador clearly have the largest populations of the 74, and they rank rather high on GNP (Lebanon near the top). However, their rankings in area are much lower. Panama, which clusters a bit later with them, has somewhat smaller population, area and GNP. Surinam, Nicaragua, Liberia, French Guiana and Iceland all have the largest territories of the micro-territories (91,000 sq. km.—142,822 sq. km.), but they have more modest populations (36,000—1,655,000) and GNP's ($9m—$567m). The first sub-cluster (Wallis-Futuna Islands, *et al*) is composed of exceedingly tiny places. Their populations range from less than 500 to 397,000; their GNP's, from less than a half million dollars to $263m; their areas, from less than one half square kilometre to 14,763 sq. km. The second sub-cluster which joins the first very quickly consists of territories whose scores on the three variables tend to be a little higher than those of the first sub-cluster.

There is a temptation to give names to each of the sub-clusters. There can be no distinctions among them as to types of polities or kinds of cultures, unless one wishes to make the unlikely assumption that culture and polity are related to size. Indeed, there is a clear lack of relationship between the sub-clusters and the independence and/or the length of independence of the territories. The independent states and the historical micro-territories are more highly concentrated in the sub-clusters of the large territories, but they are scattered throughout.

One final caveat is in order. The addition of other size variables, e.g., agricultural area, urban population or steel consumption, each with its own theoretical assumptions, would have changed the picture. The outcome depends not only upon the method of clustering adopted and the essentially arbitrary choice of clustering value, but also upon the decision to use three and only three size variables and to treat each of them as equally important.

B. Statehood and its Determinants

Each of the 222 territories with which this analysis began had sufficient identity to be considered a separate political system or sub-system of one kind or another. Each, therefore, possessed one aspect of statehood: a legal and administrative system common to and distinct for a territory. Statehood, however, also implies independence or sovereignty, i.e., the location of ultimate decision-making power within the polity itself. Independence, hence full statehood, is clearly related to size.

Almost all of the larger territories of the world are, since 1960, sovereign. Of the 107 listed by name in Table IX (the non-micro-territories), only three are by international legal definition dependent.[7] Of the 74 micro-territories, on the other hand, only 24 are independent, and this independence for some is minimal. For example, Liechtenstein maintains its "sovereignty" in the sense that it can request Switzerland to return the responsibility for its foreign affairs and currency. Still, this right is important if Liechtenstein is compared with Guam, which cannot unilaterally decide the same for itself.

Territories, of course, can be dichotomized into sovereign and non-sovereign entities only in legal terms. Many smaller places have been able to find means of self-determination without managing all of their own affairs. Liechtenstein has its agreement with Switzerland; the Vatican and Monaco have similar arrangements with Italy and France. Each, however, is called sovereign. Other small territories have worked out relationships with larger polities in which the smaller partner does not claim a separate sovereignty but is to all intents and purposes free to make most of its own decisions or to participate fully in those of the larger polity. Surinam and the Netherlands Antilles are autonomous and equal parts of the Kingdom of the Netherlands. Antigua, Dominica, Grenada, St. Kitts-Nevis-Anguilla and St. Lucia are states in association with the United Kingdom. The Cook Islands form a self-governing territory in special association with New Zealand. Guadeloupe, French Guiana, Martinique and Réunion are departments of France, and as such send deputies to the National Assembly in Paris. Of the 74 micro-territories, 13 are in this category.

Six of the territories are protectorates and another 31 are colonies, unincorporated territories, overseas territories, etc. These have in common the characteristic that their future can be determined legally only by their respective metropoles. However, they range all the way from those ruled tightly from a far-away capital to those with a great deal of internal self-control.

Almost two thirds of the micro-territories have legally sanctioned arrangements that, at the moment, please their inhabitants. In Table XI along the rows, these 74 territories are divided into independent states, associated states and protectorates and colonies. Along the columns they are divided into those in which the predominant sentiment is to be happy with independence if it has been attained, or to desire it if not, those in which this sentiment is in favour of associated status or incorporation, whether attained or not, and those in which there is either no active objection to their dependent status or a desire for only gradual political

[7] These are Angola, Hong Kong and Puerto Rico. Other dependent territories with populations over one million, not included in Table IX because of lack of economic data, are Mozambique and Papua/New Guinea.

evolution.[8] It is not surprising that independent peoples do not want to lose their independence, but it is noteworthy that inhabitants of almost one third of the dependent territories want either to maintain their present status or to develop only slowly away from it. Most of the remaining territories have movements for some form of association with the metropole, and only three wish true independence.

What are the differences between territories in which people want independence, those in which they want association with some larger polity and those in which they prefer a more gradual political development? Above, we demonstrated an association between size and independence, i.e., that larger territories are far more likely to be independent than are smaller territories.

Then we showed that non-independent peoples of smaller territories frequently prefer some form of association to complete independence; they are likely to think of themselves as less capable of independent existence than are populations of larger territories. From those observations, therefore, it appears that a threshold exists beyond which peoples perceive independence as the only proper form of political existence but before which they may be willing to work out other arrangements. The option for independence or for other arrangements below the threshold is not strongly related to size. The results of an analysis of variance[9]

[8] Data on "predominant sentiment" were gathered from the clippings files of UNITAR. A relatively strong movement without significant opposition was sufficient to place the territory in one category or another. In the absence of such a movement, statements by indigenous leaders were used. If nothing of this nature was reported, it was assumed that the inhabitants were reasonably happy with whatever arrangements they had.

[9] Variance is the arithmetic mean of the sum of the squared deviations from the mean of scores on some variable (e.g., population) for some group of units (e.g., territories), i.e.,

$$\text{variance} = \frac{\sum_{i=1}^{n} (X_i - \bar{X})^2}{n}$$

where n = the number of units, $\bar{X}$ = the mean of the units' scores on some variable and X_i = the score of a particular unit. For example, to determine variance of population for the 74 micro-territories, we calculate the mean or average population, find the difference between that figure and the population of each of the 74 territories, square each of these differences, add up these results and divide by 74 (the number of territories).

Variances can be calculated for sub-sets of the 74 territories, however. In fact, we can measure the variance within each of the three groups of territories as divided by political self-perceptions in Table XI. We can also measure variance among the means of the three groups. The greater the variance of, e.g., population between the three groups as compared with its variance within them, the greater is the probability of a relationship between size of population and kind of political self-perception. By dividing the estimate of between variance by the estimate of within variance, we obtain a statistic (F) which, when compared with

TABLE XI—MICRO-TERRITORIES BY LEGAL STATUS AND POLITICAL SELF-PERCEPTION

	Territories already independent or where a pro-independence movement is strong	Territories where majority opinion seems to favour association	Territories where majority opinion seems to favour status quo or slow political evolution	Totals
Independent states	24	0	0	24
Associated states	0	13	0	13
Protectorates and colonies	3	21	13	37
Totals	27	34	13	74

indicate only a weak association between population and GNP, on the one hand, and the categories of political self-perception, on the other, within the 74 micro-territories.

For population and self-perceptions, $r_i = .35$
For GNP and self-perceptions, $r_i = .33$

(on a scale ranging from .00 to 1.00, from complete lack of association between size and political self-perception to complete correlation between them).[10] This means that insofar as the relationship holds, the more people or wealth a territory has, the more likely its people are to think of

---

a table of expected values, suggests whether this relationship could be expected by simple chance more frequently than one time out of a hundred (or at any other level of probability we wish to set).

The F-test only guides one's judgement in deciding whether or not a relationship exists. How strong the relationship is, if it exists, can be measured by an intra-class correlation coefficient (r_i). This coefficient measures the degree of homogeneity (e.g., of populations) within the groups relative to the total variability (e.g., of populations of all of the 74 territories). It is found as follows:

$$r_i = \frac{V_b - V_w}{V_b + (\bar{n} - 1) V_w}$$

where V_b = the between estimate of variance, V_w = the within estimate of variance and $\bar{n}$ = the average number of territories in each type.

[10] Technically, r_i may go below .00 if all the variation takes place within groups and the means among groups are equal. This is rarely found in practice. Zero is the value of r_i if the groups are as homogeneous, as would be expected by chance when there is no relationship.

themselves as having the right to a separate political life from any larger entity. The relationship between area and self-perception, however, is not even statistically significant; it could easily be the result of pure chance.

If self-perceptions in micro-territories are only weakly related to size, are they more closely associated with location? Two indexes of location are based upon the distance in miles from the micro-territories to the centres of population. One measures the distance to the capital or major city of the nearest country of two million or more inhabitants. The second measures the distance to the nearest world capital: London, Moscow or New York. The former is an attempt to capture the degree of isolation within a regional context, whereas the latter is an effort to get at isolation in a more universal context. These measures correlate with the political categories only weakly:

For distance to the nearest state of two million people and self-perception, $r_i = .26$

For distance to the nearest world capital and self-perception, $r_i = .14$

(again using a scale ranging from .00 to 1.00).

The group means indicate that the further a territory is from one of the population centres, the less is the probability that its people will think of themselves as constituting an appropriate population unit for separate political existence. Perhaps this is opposite of what might intuitively be expected. Nevertheless, political self-perceptions are only weakly influenced by location, at least measured in miles. Results might be very different if data were available for measuring ease of transportation, degree and content of communication patterns and psychological identifications.

An alternative measure of the potential independence of micro-territories is the degree to which their government budgets are subsidized by other governments. Indeed, this measure may be a more objective indication of the territory's ability to go it alone than are the beliefs of its people. Unfortunately, data on subsidies are available only for 26 territories.[11] The percentage of government budget originating from outside the territory is correlated[12] with

[11] These data are reported in Patricia Wohlgemuth Blair, *The Ministate Dilemma* (New York, Carnegie Endowment for International Peace. Occasional Paper No. 6, October, 1967).

[12] Since the dependent variable, subsidy, as well as the independent variables of size and location are measured in interval scales, it is possible to use a stronger measure of relationship than the intra-class correlation coefficient. The product moment correlation coefficient (r) measures the co-variation of two variables. In analysis of variance, where one of the variables, political self-perception of groups, is measured in a nominal scale, it is impossible to calculate co-variation if the latter is defined as

$$\sum_{i=1}^{n} (X_i - \overline{X})(Y_i - \overline{Y})$$

Population	$r = -.32$
Area	$r = -.28$
GNP	$r = -.48$
Distance to nearest populous country	$r = .18$
Distance to nearest world capital	$r = .10$

In so far as there is a relationship between location and subsidy, the more isolated is the territory, the greater is the amount of funds it needs from elsewhere. The relationship between subsidy and size, specially economic size, is stronger. The larger the territory, the smaller is the percentage subsidy (see table XII).

C. Conclusion

There are many ways to identify the micro-states of the world. The use of any single variable, however, is too narrow in its conception. Moreover, one's arbitrary judgment probably plays a greater rôle in the determination of cut-off points when only one variable is used than when several are involved. Nevertheless, in either case, the decision as to where to separate micros and macros is not automatic, but must rely upon the theoretical criteria of the researcher. Moreover, the measures to denote size must be carefully selected and weighed *vis-à-vis* one another. Perhaps in future research, additional measures and refinements of those in this paper could be used to provide a more sensitive grouping of micro-territories. Even so, the use of the three most obvious measures of territorial size, weighted equally, seem to be sufficient for drawing up a workable listing.

Let $\overline{X}$ stand for mean population and $\overline{Y}$ for mean subsidy; X_i then represents the score of a particular territory on population and Y_i represents its score on subsidy. By finding these differences between territorial scores and the average for all of the territories, by multiplying the two differences and by summing, we get the co-variation between population size and subsidy size. Since the value of co-variation can be much greater than unity, it is convenient to divide by the square root of the product of the variation in the two variables. Therefore:

$$r = \frac{\sum\limits_{i=1}^{n} (X_i - \overline{X})(Y_i - \overline{Y})}{\sqrt{[\sum (X - \overline{X})^2][\sum (Y - \overline{Y})^2]}}$$

Values of r then run between -1.0 to $+1.0$, i.e., from total negative correlation to total positive correlation.

The product moment correlation coefficient may also be considered a measure of the deviation of the points in a scattergram from the linear least squares regression line. If the territories are plotted by subsidy and population, one straight line can be determined from which the sums of the squares of the distances to each point is at a minimum. The slope of this regression line indicates the nature of the linear relationship between the two variables. A high correlation coefficient indicates that most of the points are on or near this line; a low coefficient indicates a more random distribution.

TABLE XII—RELATIONSHIP BETWEEN LOCATION, SELF-PERCEPTION AND SUBSIDY

Territory	Self-per-ception*	Subsidy	Miles to capital of nearest state of 2 million	Miles to London, Moscow or New York
American Samoa	C	90%	2,100	7,000
Antigua	A	84%	300	1,750
Bahamas	A	—	300	1,100
Bahrein	A	—	300	2,100
Barbados	I	—	550	2,050
Bermuda	A	—	850	850
British Honduras	A	81%	250	1,900
Brunei	A	—	850	5,300
Cape Verde Islands	I	—	550	2,750
Cayman Islands	C	73%	250	1,500
Comoro Archipelago	A	—	550	4,550
Cook Islands	A	54%	2,050	6,600
Cyprus	I	—	150	1,350
Dominica	A	29%	350	1,900
El Salvador	I	—	150	2,000
Equatorial Guinea	I	—	200	3,250
Falkland Islands	C	1%	1,150	6,350
Fiji Islands	A	—	1,700	7,700
French Guiana	A	—	1,400	2,800
French Polynesia	A	23%	2,550	6,150
French Territory of the Afars and Issas	A	—	300	3,000
The Gambia	I	—	100	2,700
Gibraltar	A	—	300	1,050
Gilbert and Ellice Is.	C	11%	2,800	7,250
Grenada	A	29%	350	2,050
Guam	A	—	1,550	5,950
Guadeloupe	A	—	300	1,800
Iceland	I	—	1,000	1,100
Jamaica	I	—	250	1,550
Kuwait	I	—	300	1,850
Lebanon	I	—	50	1,450
Lesotho	I	—	200	5,750
Liechtenstein	I	—	100	550
Liberia	I	—	200	3,100
Luxembourg	I	—	50	250
Macao	A	—	1,150	4,250
Malta	I	—	200	1,200
Martinique	A	—	400	1,950

* Political self-perception is coded as follows: I = independent territories or territories in which there is a strong independence movement. A = territories which are now associated with a larger policy or in which the people would like such association. C = colonies in which there is a desire to maintain the *status quo* or to evolve very slowly.

TABLE XII—(continued)

Territory	Self-per-ception*	Subsidy	Miles to capital of nearest state of 2 million	Miles to London, Moscow or New York
Mauritius and Dependencies	I	—	700	5,520
Monaco	I	—	400	600
Montserrat	C	52%	250	1,800
Nauru	I	—	2,550	7,500
Netherlands Antilles	A	—	200	1,950
New Caledonia	A	—	1,300	8,000
New Hebrides	C	—	1,650	8,100
Nicaragua	I	—	150	2,100
Niue Island	C	60%	1,900	7,200
Trust Territory of the Pacific Islands	A	89%	2,900	6,450
Panama	I	—	450	2,200
Pitcairn Island	C	—	3,150	5,700
Qatar	A	—	300	2,100
Réunion	A	—	500	5,250
San Marino	I	—	150	700
Sao Tomé and Principe	I	—	400	3,450
Seychelles	A	29%	1,100	4,200
Sikkim	A	—	300	3,000
Singapore	I	—	200	5,100
Solomon Islands	C	—	2,000	7,600
St. Helena	C	60%	1,350	4,550
St. Kitts	A	26%	250	1,750
St. Lucia	A	26%	450	1,950
St. Pierre-et-Miquelon	A	—	900	900
St. Vincent	A	24%	400	2,000
Surinam	A	—	500	2,600
Swaziland	I	26%	100	5,500
Tokelau Islands	C	96%	2,300	6,800
Tonga	A	—	1,400	7,550
Trinidad and Tobago	I	—	400	2,200
Turks and Caicos	C	73%	200	1,300
Vatican	I	—	—	850
Virgin Islands (UK)	C	87%	250	1,300
Virgin Islands (USA)	A	—	150	1,600
Wallis and Futuna	A	—	1,950	7,350
Western Samoa	I	—	2,100	7,200

* Political self-perception is coded as follows: I = independent territories or territories in which there is a strong independence movement. A = territories which are now associated with a larger policy or in which the people would like such association. C = colonies in which there is a desire to maintain the *status quo* or to evolve very slowly.

It is not enough, however, to locate small systems and sub-systems. What is to distinguish Tangier Island in the Chesapeake or Tory Island off Ireland from Nauru or Pitcairn? Easily, the answer is that a distinct political system of its own allows a territory to be considered a micro-state. But what is a distinct political system? The answer to this question must be broad enough to allow more than a dichotomy between sovereign states and colonies. An increasing number of governments in small territories are seeking a form of self-determination somewhere between the two. Indeed, if the measures were available, it might be found that the degrees of independence of micro-territories could best be described by a continuum running from a situation in which almost no major decisions are made within the territory to one in which almost as many are made as in much larger states.

People in some micro-territories want greater power over their political destinies than do inhabitants of other territories. There seems to some slight relationship between isolation and less independence and a somewhat greater relationship between larger size and more independence. Yet the questions implicit at the beginning of the paper—how small and isolated does a territory have to be before its people realize that they cannot take care of themselves—does not seem to be an appropriate one in view of these findings. The variables with greater explanatory power are probably political and/or psychological in nature.

Micro-states and territories constitute a "micro-cosmos" as historical and as varied as the "macro-cosmos." Their problems are no more amenable to some general set of answers than are those of their larger counterparts.

INDEX

Aden, 31, 43
Alaska
  self-determination of, 26
  United States of America and, 26, 83
Alker, 43
Allenstein plebiscite (1920), 24
America, *see* United States of America
American Samoa, 49, 165*n*
  United States of America and, 63
  Western Samoa and, 110-111
Andorra, 78
  emergence of, 49
  political stability of, 54
Angola, 17, 92, 195*n*
  Cabinda and, 66
  Portugal and, 66
Anguilla, 55, 69, 165
Antarctic Territories, 81
Antarctic Treaty (1959), 81
Antigua, 26
  Barbuda and, 55, 165
  United Kingdom and, 68, 195
  in West Indies Associated States, 95-96
  in West Indies Federation, 93
Argentina and the Falkland Islands (Malvinas), 56, 61, 127
Ascension, 49
Australia
  Christmas Island and, 65

Cocos (Keeling) Islands and, 63
military bases of, 146-147
Nauru and, 86
Norfolk Island and, 65
Papua and, 61

Bahamas
  United Kingdom and, 62
  United Nations technical aid to, 175
Bahrein
  international organization membership of, 113*n*
  United Kingdom and, 69
  United Nations specialized agency membership of, 137
    FAO associate membership of, 143
    UNESCO associate membership of, 143
    WHO membership of, 140
Barbados, 43, 49, 76
  independence of, 95
  United Nations and, 119
    ILO observer of, 140
    United Nations specialized agency membership of, 136
  in West Indies Federation, 93
Barbuda and Antigua, 55, 165
Basutoland, *see* Lesotho
Bechuanaland, *see* Botswana